SCIENCE AND TECHNOLOGY IN COLONIAL INDIA

Kamlesh Mohan

AAKAR

Science and Technology in Colonial India
Kamlesh Mohan

First Published, 2014

ISBN 978-93-5002-280-1

Published by
AAKAR BOOKS
28 E Pocket IV, Mayur Vihar Phase I, Delhi 110 091
Phone : 011 2279 5505 Telefax : 011 2279 5641
info@aakarbooks.com; www.aakarbooks.com

Printed at
Saurabh Printers Pvt. Ltd., A 16, Sector IV, Noida

Contents

Acknowledgements vii

Preface ix

Introduction 1

1. The Colonial Ethnography: Imperial Pursuit of Knowledge for Hegemony in British India (Late Nineteenth to Early Twentieth Century) 29
2. The Development of Modern Sciences in the Punjab University under Colonial Rule, 1882-1947 68
3. Technology and Religion: Recasting Hindu Consciousness Through Print in India with Special Reference to the Punjab During the Nineteenth Century 105
4. Ruchi Ram Sahni and the Pursuit of Science in a Colonial Society 133

Index 155

Acknowledgements

I wish to thank editors of books and journals wherein the following articles had been published:

1. 'Colonial Ethnography: Imperial Pursuit of Knowledge for Hegemony in British India' was presented at the 19th International Union of History of Philosophy and Science Congress, Zaragoza (Spain), August 22-29, 1993.
2. 'The Development of Modern Sciences in Punjab University under Colonial Rule 1882-1947' in Uma Das Gupta ed. *Science and Modern India: An Institutional History 1784-1947*, PHISPC, Vol XVI (Delhi: Pearson, 2010-11).
3. 'Ruchi Ram Sahni: Pursuit of Science in the Colonial Society', in Narender K. Sehgal, Satpal Sangwan and Subodh Mahanti eds., *Uncharted Terrains* (Delhi: Vigyan Prasar, Ministry of Science and Technology, 2000).
4. 'Technology and Religion: Recasting Hindu Consciousness Through Print in India with Special Reference to the Punjab During the Nineteenth Century', in *Archives International Histoire Des Sciences*, Estrto Dal n. 147, Vol. 51, 2001.

It was originally presented at the International Congress on History of Philosophy and Science in Liege (Belgium), August 1999.

Kamlesh Mohan

Preface

Writing this book was both an exciting venture and a learning experience. The study of the process of transfer of European scientific knowledge (originally born out of human concerns and needs) and its product technology from Britain, its diffusion and manipulation for social and political control as well as maximum resource-extraction yielded a few insights. One is that scientific method undergoes change with the development of new branches of science. Secondly, Indian perception of science and technology was based not on what the British did in Britain but what the British did to India. However, a comparative perspective of their utilisation for socio-economic development in the mother country was always instructive. Pandit Madan Mohan Malaviya's evidence before the Indian Industrial Commission 1916-18 is an incisive commentary on the skewed institutionalisation of science in India and its harmful and long-term implications for the Indian economy as well as for its political and moral debility. The imperial engagement with instruction of the Indian people in science and execution of technological projects (e.g. railways, irrigation and uniform postal system) wittingly or unwittingly struck at the core values of the Indian epistemological tradition and seared its multicultural fabric to a great extent.

As a student of the social history of science, I realised that there is a close relationship between politics and knowledge in any of the disciplines, e.g. science, literature and arts. It's conceptualisation and exposition became fairly sophisticated in the hands of colonial ideologues, administrators and scientists (often described as 'scientific soldiers'). In fact, science was politics by other means.

In the course of my research and writing a number of scholars, students and veteran teachers who had participated in international and weekly seminars, organised by various colleges in the Universities of Oxford and Cambridge from 1993-96, enabled me to sharpen my arguments. I express my heartfelt thanks for their valuable suggestions and comments on my lecture in Maison de Sciences De L' Homme (Paris) as a visiting professor in 2001 (these have been incorporated in the chapter on colonial ethnography.

Professor R.P. Bambah, former Vice-Chancellor, Panjab University, helped me to get a balanced perspective on the development of modern sciences in the university through detailed discussions and access to his personal collection of documents and books about Sarvadaman Chawla and Government College, Lahore (Pakistan), Prof. Ashok Sahni's insights and long association with the university kept me on the proper track. Ms. Uma Sood alias Kamini Kaushal provided me with rare writings of her father, Shiv Ram Kashyap. Dr. Subodh Mahanty, Scientist, Vigyan Prasar, Sujata Samant nee, Mahanty and Dr. S.K. Sahni, Indian National Science, Academy sent me material on the life and career of many scientists.

I deeply appreciate Professor K.N. Pathak former Vice-Chancellor for his graciousness in granting me academic leave whenever required. My profound gratitude to Dr. A.R. Kidwai, former member and chairperson, Union Public Service Commission, former Professor and Head, Department of Chemistry and Dean, Faculty of Sciences, Aligarh Muslim University (1951-67) for sharing valuable information regarding Piara Singh Gill's contribution. My work would not have been completed without the archival material provided by Professor Ashgar Nadeem, Government College University, Lahore and by Shazia Moghal, Researcher, Punjab Archives, Lahore (Pakistan).

Last but not the least is my debt to institutions, namely British Library (London), Panjab University Library

(Chandigarh) Nehru Memorial Museum & Library and Arya Pratinidhi Sabha Sansthan (New Delhi) for providing me with facilities to consult their collection of books, microfilms, private papers and oral interviews with prominent men and women.

I can never thank my father Shri K.L. Zakir adequately for sharing my burden of proof-reading and removing ambiguities in expression. By overlooking my lapses in fulfilling social obligations in the course of my research and writing, he enabled me to focus on my work.

As these essays have been written in different contexts, some repetition was bound to occur for the sake of clarity. I seek the indulgence of readers of the book on this issue.

Finally, I thank Shri K.K. Saxena, Aakar Books, Delhi for showing endless patience and concern for meticulous printing and impressive getup of this book.

I take responsibility for any lapses and mistakes in the book.

Chandigarh
February 10, 2014

Kamlesh Mohan

Introduction

The present book tries to explore some aspects of the socio-political history of science and technology in colonial India. In the course of discussion, it refers not merely to the British motives and goals of incorporating the component of scientific knowledge technology in their administrative and educational policy and using it for territorial expansion and development of 'technologies of governance' but also to the accompanying culture. It entails a discussion of significant issues such as the character of their transfer from imperialist Britain to India, mechanisms of their diffusion and response of Indians, especially intellectuals.

Recent studies on imperialism and colonialism have shown that these two terms no longer connote merely political and economic domination of one country over the other. Having strong ideological underpinnings and a variety of strategies, the making of the British empire and construction of the colonial state in India was a long and complex process. It was coeval with the transfer of scientific knowledge, development of technologies of governance as well as of mapping their empire and composing an ethnographic picture of the subject society through population surveys, census reports and handbooks on those social groups which posed a threat to the stability of the newly-built empire. The process of colonising the Indian consciousness was an integral part of the imperialist strategy for hegemony.

The task of unravelling this multi-layered process must keep in view the fact of the prolonged cultural encounter at many levels between India and Britain. It implicated a keen contest of two cultures including their religious, literary and scientific traditions of knowledge, techniques, ideologies of governance as well as modes and relations of production. As a multifaceted historical phenomenon, the issue of cultural encounter remained an undercurrent in the entire career of imperialist rule in India. Owing to the complexity of themes taken up in the present book, I have taken the liberty of writing a rather long introduction describing features of the progress of science and technology under the East India Company and the Crown rule.

During the 1960s and 70s, a number of scholarly studies have debated the issues of transmission of Western scientific knowledge, mechanisms of its diffusion, its positive moral impact as well as material and modernising implications of technological projects, e.g. irrigation, railways, telegraph and uniform postal system from the Euro-centric perspective primarily. Their studies revolved around the standard trope of civilising mission in the former colonial countries. These scholars put forth a two-pronged justification: (i) science as a catalytic agent in the lives of the Eastern people, who were immersed in dense superstitions; (ii) as an indispensable replacement of the ancient and primitive techniques and tools by modern technological artifacts and methods. Thus, modernisation has been projected as the component as well as a function of Western scientific knowledge and technology.

During the 1980s and 90s, content and context of the academic discourse changed owing to the recognition of a close relationship between science and politics.[1] Without denying the emancipatory potentialities of science, it was realised that the colonial state's policies in Africa and Asia had retarded the diffusion and utilisation of scientific knowledge for promoting their capitalistic interests and not for solving the socio-economic problems of the people. A critique of the colonial state's science policy and the related institutional structures began to take shape with the emergence and growth of the nationalist struggles. A multiplicity of voices contributed to the making of its complex and rich tapestry. The post-colonial scholarship about the non-West dealt with the problem of politics of knowledge from two perspectives: historical and new sociology of science. The common feature in their writings on the theory of science was the emphasis on its local and social context. Elaborating this point, Bhaskar Roy has remarked that science must be conceptualised "as a social process, irreducible to an individual acquisition, whose aim is the production of the knowledge of the mechanisms of the production of phenomenon in nature...."

Steven Yearley, a sociologist of science, has also conceded the relevance of social factors but not of ontological idealism which forms an integral part of constructive perspective. In his view, a combination of 'constructive' insights with the political-economy approach is more practical and effective in studying the development of science and technology.[2] It may be pointed out that too many theories, propounded by the sociologists of science, have led to the total neglect of historical questions regarding the origin and growth of science from the seventeenth century onwards. Joseph Needham's multivolume work *Science and Civilization in China* (1954 -)[3] has demonstrated the immense value of historical approach and comparative perspective. His discussions of particular scientific and technological innovations, which were transmitted from India to China through the spread of Buddhism, must be kept in view while evaluating the Western claim regarding its constant superiority in science and technology. In his recent work on the transmission of scientific knowledge, a Japanese scholar has argued that the centres for science were constantly shifting.[4] Another scholar has enriched the argument by his observation that an essential precondition for the growth of knowledge was innovation and transformation, produced through the process of perpetual transfer of knowledge from one region to another.[5] Besides, the Western ideological assumption that only the exceptionally-gifted individuals, belonging to elite groups, could produce knowledge,[6] sounds racist and unconvincing. Rejection of this assumption has brought two-fold recognition: (i) that scientific knowledge and technologies, produced by a variety of social groups in the former colonies, contributed to the evolution of knowledge and thus not inferior; (ii)that imperialist projection of Indians being incapable of pursuing 'pure sciences' was a deliberate ploy to confine them to low-paid back-breaking jobs as labourers in plantations, as technicians and field-workers or assistants to surveyors. Its significant outcome was to motivate historians of science to identify new actors who had participated in the production of indigenous knowledge and techniques in various fields. Thus, the radical thinkers among sociologists and historians of science in the 1980s and 90s tried to evolve a new paradigm that scientific activity in the colonial countries was neither subordinate nor dependent on the metropolitan science. They were not merely supplying new information and data but also unfamiliar botanical plants for adaptation and acclimatisation for the storehouse of Kew Gardens, mineral and agricultural products for processing, refining and for making finished articles for export to the colonies. Even more significant was their contribution in providing models of institutions for research in science and technology as well as statistical techniques for constructing class-hierarchies in Britain.

The process of the introduction and instutionalisation of Western science in colonial India was neither smooth nor uncontested. After an initial phase of conflict and disagreement between the Court of Directors in London and the representatives of the East India Company in Calcutta over the issue of seemingly unproductive financial investment on the transfer and utilisation of Western science and technology, the decision was made in its favour. Besides being an aid for territorial expansion and integration and a solution for boosting the Company's rapidly depleting revenues, other reasons and circumstances have been highlighted by Russel Dionne and Roy MacLeod. They observed:

> Unique problems and special needs in India when combined with circumstances initially peculiar to its rule made the subcontinent a testing ground for ideas and institutions which were emerging in Britain around the turn of the century.[7]

They further added that political and climatic conditions existed in India which warranted the extension of state-sponsored scientific activities on an unprecedented scale. The size of India necessitated the integration of efforts by a large number of technical personnel.[8] It resulted in a planned scientific and technical programme but not a system. Finally, as a testing ground for state-sponsored application of science and technology projects, India provided a 'vast storehouse'[9] of information from which other parts of the empire could borrow and benefit.

These factors acquired special relevance in the context of the prevailing Western faith in the efficacy of science as an instrument and mode of knowledge and also as an administrative method for devising solutions for the practical problems of the empire. One of the major problems was to develop the 'technologies of governance' in the fast-expanding territorial possessions of a trading company. In the context of colonial India, Ainslie Embree has argued that the mapping and demarcation of clearly defined territorial boundaries was one of the key factors contributing to the transformation of a 'trading company into a state'.[10]

Such concerns had underpinned the Company's decision to undertake detailed and well-organised surveys. These were rooted in the belief that territory and knowledge intersect each other. Elaborating this idea, Mathew H. Edney observed, "After 1750, military and civilian officials of the East India Company launched a massive intellectual campaign to transform a land of incomprehensible spectacle into an empire of knowledge."[11] One of the front-runners in this campaign were the geographers, who engaged themselves in a number of activities, grouped under the banner 'field-sciences'. They mapped the landscapes, studied the inhabitants, collected geological and botanical specimens during the seventeenth and eighteenth centuries.[12] The important point made by Edney is that all the surveys and maps, which the British made in the first hundred years of their ascendancy, signified their evolving conceptions of what India should be.[13] They mapped the India that they imagined, perceived and governed. It also reflected the relationship between the goals and extent as well as the nature of the British control over the Indian territories.[14] This particular issue determined the geographical or territorial configuration and nature of representation of India in James Rennell's *Map of Hindoostan* (1782) and an accompanying volume of *Memoirs* (1783). Despite the fact that the process of constituting 'British India' remained in motion till the acquisition of control over Madras, Maharashtra (1818), Upper India and the Lahore Kingdom (1849) and legislation of the Interpretation Act in 1889[15] by the British Parliament, Rennell's contribution through a variety of surveys has two-fold significance: (i) it promoted the "development and refinement of the colonial administrative apparatus as well as of the colonial state; (ii) his work also contributed substantially to the nascent scientific discourse of geography and geology in nineteenth Europe. "In the theoretical debates of the nineteenth century", observes Zaheer Baber, "geographers and geologists in Britain and continental Europe drew extensively on Rennell's work, especially his study of ocean currents, undertaken on the return voyage from India."[16] The British imperialists, apart from delineating geographical boundaries of 'British India', were seriously engaged in the project of textual production on Indian classical languages, land and various components of population around the axis of religion, caste and tribes, literature, science, philosophy and culture which took the form of three projects.[17] All these projects were an integral part of the larger imperial project: consolidation of the British rule through gradual centralisation of colonial knowledge and administrative practice. Its definition and scope had been broadened by the third decade of the nineteenth century when the British decided to govern their colonies, especially India not only politically but also epistemologically.[18] Changes in the general orientation of scientific knowledge in Europe, which were linked with the growth of interest in social statistics, implicated collection of detailed information about population with reference to physical features of land. It played an important role in drawing attention to the complex internal structure of colonial societies from mid-nineteenth century onwards. A strong concern with imperial documentation of the special characteristics of population was intimately associated with the emergence of the modern nation-state which could use social statistics in order "to govern effectively in a rational and conscious manner."[19] E.J. Hobsbawm's empasis on the "element of artifact, invention and social engineering, which enters into the making of nations"[20], was incorporated into surveys, conducted throughout the nineteenth century in India. These surveys reflected not only "shifts in the orientation of scientific knowledge" but also "changes in the material and practical requirements of a colonial state in the making."[21] Implicit in this development was the epistemological shift from religion to science, which enabled the colonial administrators and policy-makers to give a racist angle to the study and representation of the 'other' in Africa and Asia. While establishing a rationalist connection between precise knowledge and social control, they initiated and formalised colonial ethnography from the 1840s to the 1930s in order to consolidate imperial 'hegemony'[22] and freeze social identities of Indians on the twin basis of religion and caste. Being increasingly aware of the bewildering complexity of the internal structure of numerous religious communities, castes and tribes and histories of their social customs, daily practices, modes of governance and laws, the British administrators-turned-ethnographers, chose the categories of 'religion' and 'caste' as the theoretical handles for rhetorical and referential purposes. These categories were deployed for objectifying the Indian people and converting them into cold statistical figures through the process of disciplinary enumeration. In her study, Rashmi Pant has analysed the far-reaching impact of the colonial ethnographic practice on the emergence of caste as a substantive category of social identity in the British census of India. She has argued that caste had to undergo a process of regimented ordering and standardisation in order to fix its status as the locus of the British census.[23] Such an exercise became mandatory for the colonial ethnographer who found the traditional caste-groupings dispersed and fluid and thus confusing.[24] Similarly, the category of religion (used only once in 1853 in the census of Great Britain) had been used as a constant referent to count and pigeonhole Hindus, Muslims and Sikhs in census reports of 1853, 1865 and 1873 for the North-Western Provinces (later designated as UP), Punjab and Bengal.

The problem of defining Hindus and Sikhs in the British Punjab remained unresolved from the mid-nineteenth century to the mid-twentieth century owing to the imperialist strategy of constructing impenetrable cultural boundaries between the two communities, having common cultural roots and family ties.[25] Herbert Risley's manipulation of scientific instruments and the prevalent racial theories in Europe to promote his anthropometric interests,[26] i.e. for constructing artificial linkages between caste, race and physical attributes of the Indian people had failed to enthuse the British Government whose primary interest was to locate the 'depressed under class' in Bengal in order to use this concept as a counter-weight to the influence of the upper caste Hindus throughout India.[27]

From the 1870s onwards, caste emerged as a more valuable category than religion in the colonial imagination. The colonial administrator-cum-ethnographer found it more suitable for classification, enumeration and social control because it embraced the whole of India and almost all segments of society. Thus, caste became a special target and site of knowledge for the last three censuses of British India, i.e. 1911, 1921 and 1931 when the question of political representation assumed importance. A thorough knowledge of the statistical composition of the subject society was regarded as an important aid in determining the 'proper' representation of different segments of population in the representative bodies at the local, provincial and central levels. Besides, caste could be more easily manipulated for controlling majorities and manipulated for controlling majorities and minorities through a number of rules and laws. Obviously, the scientific method was increasingly deployed to ensure that no particular group could monopolise power.

Regarding the value of this qualified and quantified information about caste in relation with a variety of data, R. Saumrez Smith has made an insightful observation. The development of administrative records and survey reports was linked with the new strategy of political control, i.e. 'Rule by records and reports' in the second half of the nineteenth century.[28] In his view, there was correspondence between the gradual construction of an official understanding of the Indian society and the gradual extension of the 'rule of law'.[29] All these issues have been discussed at length in the Chapter 'Colonial Ethnography: Imperial Pursuit of Knowledge for Hegemony in British India.'

The preceding discussion has shown that science and technology transferred from Britain and used for carrying out extensive programmes of executing trigonometrical, topographical, hydrographic, geodetic and geological surveys in India were geared to ensure military, administrative and economic control of the subcontinent. Ethnographic, population and linguistic surveys from the mid-nineteenth to the mid-twentieth century facilitated extension of imperialist control of the human resources through their division into the categories of religion and caste. Under the banner of the Asiatic Society of Bengal, the Orientalists led by Sir William Jones had already conquered the epistemological space. Through their explorations into the rich biodiversity of the subcontinent, the British botanists had appropriated the natural world at regional and all-India levels, leading to the establishment of a number of botanical gardens in the eighteenth century. The Royal Botanical Gardens in Calcutta, like the Royal Asiatic Society, provided the nucleus for a number of scientific societies and organisations that included among others the Royal Horticultural Society of India, the Agricultural Department of India and the Forest Department. In addition, it played a crucial role in "The international transfer of plants of economic, commercial and medicinal value across continents in the late nineteenth century".[30] Another important outcome of the botanical gardens was the graduation of the amateur explorer and collector of plants into a professional botanist whose researches advanced the production of new botanical knowledge.[31]

In the entire process of the production of colonial knowledge, Indians had been placed in a hierarchical relationship with the British. They were neither trusted for their ability and integrity nor given an equal status in the colonial scientific societies and organisations/institutions. I shall cite two examples to illustrate my point. First is the Asiatic Society of Bengal, founded and inaugurated in January 1784 by Sir William Jones, a judge at the Supreme Court and a versatile scholar.[32] It may be pointed out that Jones' specific goals in establishing this Society to 'Study of Man and Nature', implicating investigation into the indigenous state of science and technology in ancient India through proficiency and mastery of its classical languages, were consistent with the original object of devising "the best mode of ruling Bengal". Besides, he sought to examine the "particular advantages to our country and mankind from our sedulous and united enquiries into history of science and art of these Asiatic regions, especially of the British dominions in India."[33] In order to achieve these ends, a number of scholars proficient in classical languages, legal experts, and practitioners of fine arts were deployed. Jones, himself acquired proficiency in Sanskrit to reduce dependence on Indian scholars and mould his interpretations in accordance with imperialist perceptions and goals of domination.[34] His Indian collaborators were more or less instruments for providing keys to unlock the treasurers of indigenous knowledge.

My second example is the Geological Survey of India (established in 1851). In the Geological Survey of India, the first Indian apprentice Ram Singh was recruited in 1873 and Kishen Singh and Hira Singh, the next year. Two of them retired as sub-assistants. P.N. Bose was the first Indian to be appointed in a graded post in 1880.[35] Why were Indians debarred from promotion to the rank of decision-makers and from opportunities to learn the essential components of surveying? Their exclusion from any meaningful roles in the government scientific organisations was the outcome of British policy. Initially, the standard argument for exclusion of Indians was the need to keep secrecy. Later on, political considerations were cited to enforce prohibition against the instruction and training of Indians in the art of any kind of surveying. The higher authorities discouraged the employment for Indians as guides in the difficult and unfamiliar terrains and their training in surveying. Any instance of violation invited strictures.[36]

It may be inferred that Indians were used as instruments

for gathering data and information or for mastering 'the command of language', to use Bernard S. Cohn's cryptic expression,[37] for the conquest of epistemological space and for procuring access to rich resources of the natural world and the mineral wealth as well as for acquiring social control. The inferior activity of data gathering was reserved for the colonial subject and the superior intellectual work of production of knowledge was the privilege of the British scientists, administrators, ethnographers and a variety of experts. Thus, scientific hierarchies were added to social-cum-racial hierarchies by the imperialist rulers.

Despite marginalisation of Indians in the government scientific organisations and in the practice of field-sciences, the need of instructing Indians in European knowledge, especially arts and sciences continued to be emphasised in the educational minutes, despatches and inquiries by various British officials and directors of the East India Company during the eighteenth and nineteenth centuries. It must be pointed out that the pragmatic approach of the Company to technical education, with its equation of science and utility,[38] was also reflected in the development of its policy of general education. Education in India was considered to be incomplete without the component of science and technology as is evident in the arguments of its advocates of various hues: evangelicals, utilitarians and technical professionals such as Royal engineers as well as business entrepreneurs. As early as 1797, Charles Grant, who was a member of the Evangelical Clapham sect and also a director of the East India Company, had thought of two different objectives. As a Christian, his concern was to prepare the Hindu mind for the reception of Christianity.[39] As a director, his advocacy of science was based on its practical advantages or utilitarian objectives, i.e. social and intellectual change implying the enlightenment of the people through the teaching of natural philosophy. Application of scientific knowledge to agriculture (for extracting the maximum revenue from land in order to resolve the financial crisis of the Company) was very important to Grant. He also believed that "skilful application of water, of fire, of steam, improvements, which would immediately concern the common people, would awaken them from their torpor, and give activity to their minds."[40] Diffusion of European knowledge, especially in science and application of technology was advocated by the Bombay Engineers Institution for the "maintenance of the British rule",[41] as is evident from the observations of S. Goodfellow, Chief Engineer of Bombay Presidency. The tenor of imperialist thinking on the purpose and great value attached to teaching of science to Indians was reflected in the task assigned to the General Committee of Public Instruction, appointed by the government in July 1823. The Committee was enjoined to suggest such measures as "...to adopt with a view to the better instruction of the people, to the introduction of useful knowledge, including the sciences and arts of Europe, and the *improvement of their normal character.*"[42] The racist mission was only one component of the rationale in the ideology of the British education policy for its colonial subjects. The second was mentioned in the dispatch of 1830 which emphasised the urgent practical necessity of teaching Indians the English language adopted as the language of public business and colonial administration.[43] The 'natives' were prepared for recruitment to lower level posts owing to their willingness to work on a paltry salary unlike the British nationals. Emergence of a new urban elite first in Bengal and later in Madras and Bombay Presidencies (as a consequence of colonial agrarian policies) and their demand for English education, especially instruction in Western science was used as an additional argument for its state-sponsored educational institutions.[44]

The policies of William Bentinck[45] and T.B. Macaulay had decisive consequences for the development and institutionalisation of Western science and technology as well as for English language, literature and arts. With his appointment as the president of the General Committee of Public Instruction in 1834, Macaulay became the aggressive spokesman of the Anglicist faction leading to the end of the dominance of the Orientalist faction which included such senior members as H.T. Prinsep and H.H. Wilson. His 'Minute on Education', announced on February 2, 1835, recommended the extension of official patronage for instruction in English and Western sciences and withdrawal of funds for education in Sanskrit, Arabic and Persian as well as for printing of literature in these languages. His rationale for not giving any encouragement to classical languages and indigenous knowledge was that it was 'an absurd history, absurd metaphysics, absurd physics'.[46] Such an adverse observation reflected the strong influence of James Mill and Charles Grant. It was also his argument for the abolition of Sanskrit College at Calcutta and *madrassa* and official patronage for state-sponsored educational institutions and the curriculum taught there.

Charles Wood's dispatch of 1854 had put the final seal on the goals and direction of development of Western science and technology as well as of educational policy for colonial India. Its objective was defined as the "diffusion of the improved arts, science, philosophy and literature of Europe, in short of European knowledge",[47] because it would

> ....secure to us a larger and more certain supply of many articles necessary for manufactures and extensively consumed by all classes of our population as well as an inexhaustible demand for the produce of British labour.[48]

In fact, instruction of Indians in European knowledge was an instrument for exploiting the human and natural resources of the country for the benefit of Britain especially for feeding its hungry machines and creating a market for its manufactured goods. Thus, there was an implicit connection between the teaching of science and making of the capitalist colonial state.

Two significant recommendations of Wood's Despatch of 1854 led to the creation of education departments in each of the provinces under the control of a central authority and founding of universities in Calcutta, Bombay and Madras in 1857. After less than three decades, the universities of Panjab, and Allahabad were established in 1882 and 1887 respectively.[49] However, these universities were no more than mere examining bodies according to the definition of their functions in Wood's Dispatch. Its recommendation for the institution of professorships in various branches of learning including science, law and languages was not implemented owing to the indifference of the British Government to the aspirations of Indians to 'do science' like Europeans and become equal partners in the production of knowledge in sciences, arts, literature and other fields.

Turning to the development of potential scientific talent of Indians through education in colleges and universities, it was not possible owing to their non-teaching character. No steps were taken to appoint professors in these universities. Indifference to the concept of scientific teaching and research continued upto 1916 when the Calcutta University College of Science and Technology was established. This example was followed by the establishment of similar postgraduate science departments in the other universities.

It is evident that the educational policy formed an integral part of the hegemonic strategies of the colonial state which had largely been dictated by imperialist perceptions and goals as well as changing needs and compulsions of the metropolis. In the chapter 'The Development of Modern Sciences in Punjab University under Colonial Rule 1882-1947', I have tried to analyse the stages of the growth of the University. Its tardy transformation from an examining and advisory body to the Punjab Government into a 'teaching corporation' by the 1920s and spectacular contribution of its alumni and teachers to the production of scientific knowledge in equal partnership with the British scientists has also been discussed. My discussion, apart from highlighting its radical difference from the older universities of India, namely, Calcutta, Madras and Bombay, has focused attention on three crucial issues: the nature and goals of the introduction, development and diffusion of Western sciences through higher education, response of Indian scientists to the tensions between the cult of rationalism inherent in the cultivation of Western science and myth-making associated with Indian religions, namely Hinduism, the conflict between the colonial agenda and the needs and aspirations of the Indian people. The response of Indian intelligentsia including creative writers, artists, teachers, technical professionals, etc. is closely linked with their perception of the relevance and functions of

Western science in an environment of politico-economic domination and cultural hegemony. Exposed to the blast of Western scientific knowledge, rationality, enlightenment philosophy and technological innovations as teachers, students and as subordinates in offices and government scientific institutions, male members (hardly any girls and women) formed their own views about functions of science. While being engaged in cultivating scientific temper, reforming or modernising their socio-religious institutions as well as practices, these men as scientists, social reformers and concerned Indians were learning new skills, concepts and ideas through discussion and analysis of the works of European thinkers and developing organisational alternatives. Their manifold initiatives and activities would provide valuable ground-work for nation-building in post-independence India.

Apart from experiencing tensions and contradictions in the peculiar socio-cultural milieu, (complicated by demographic mobility of village literati and rich peasants to towns and cities), many Indian intellectuals became increasingly conscious of the grievous burden of foreign domination and of humiliation owing to deprivation of their rights as citizens. Their creativity and leadership roles depended firstly upon their perception and intensity of their awareness of their altered circumstances, produced by the powerful colonial state's policies. Secondly, these depended upon the extent of their dissatisfaction with the traditional pattern of socio-cultural institutions and institutionalised religion as well as upon the intensity of their resentment and apprehensions aroused by the colonial hegemonisation through cultural and intellectual engineering.[50] Claims of superiority as a 'white race' in terms of physical power, resources and scientific knowledge by the colonial state, which had co-opted science to dismiss epistemologies of the Asian countries depended upon their resentment further on. These issues have been discussed in the chapter 'Ruchi Ram Sahni and the Pursuit of Science in a Colonial Society.'

On the positive side, feelings of anger and resentment against the politico-economics and cultural hegemonisation among the sensitive Indian intelligentsia crystallised into a complex response. It led to introspection and intensive search for historical guidelines from the past to cope with the present. The major purpose of this exercise was to evaluate the role of Western scientific knowledge and technologies for social change (often equated with economic development of the country). The Indian response took three forms. The first was almost total disavowal of indigenous cultural and scientific traditions and acceptance of Western learning. The second consisted of selective borrowing of ideas from the West and their incorporation into the process of adaptation and revitalisation of the Indian tradition of learning. The third was an attempt to establish the parity (even superiority) of the components of scientific knowledge in ancient India with those of the West through its retrieval and assertion. It was represented by Swami Dayanand who expounded the ideology of Arya Samaj in 1877 and institutionalised it during the 1880s in the course of his propaganda through the printed word.

In order to understand the dynamics of the ideological fermentation in the nineteenth century and its implications for the modernisation of the knowledge systems in India, I would briefly delineate the role of sensitive intellectuals who tried to evaluate the meanings of colonial modernity and redefine or adapt it in accordance with their perception of its relevance for a multi-religious society.

An indication of the appreciation of the advantages of science and technology is available in the opinions and views of Mirza Ghalib,[51] Altaf Hussain Hali, Master Ram Chandra, Munshi Zakaullah, Maulana Imdad Ali, Syed Ahmed Khan, Mumtaz Ali, Pandit Harsukh Rai and others who advocated a new intellectual approach to the problems of daily life and religion. Irrespective of their beliefs, all of them had acknowledged the adventurous spirit of the European scientists and their contribution to the advancement of knowledge of the natural world, physical sciences and medicine as well as to the development of new theoretical frameworks and methodologies. For example, Hali (1837-1914), in his *Musaddas,* described the potential role and power of modern science in building civilisation and human progress. In his view, science was an instrument in the hands of craftsmen to improve their tools and their lifestyle. By using it as a weapon, the people could fight against superstitions and outdated social mores.[52] As a relentless crusader for scientific rationality, Syed Ahmed Khan observed, "We now live in a new age, the age of scepticism in which nothing can be accepted as true unless it satisfies human reason."[53] Raja Ram Mohan Roy, (1772-1833) too had underlined the relevance of 'real useful knowledge',[54] grounded in science and fit for application to industry, for economic and social development in nineteenth century India.

Such an intense intellectual realisation regarding the diffusion of Western scientific knowledge and technologies among the people led to the establishment of a number of scientific and institutions in various provinces of the British India in mid-nineteenth century. The pioneering efforts made by the Delhi College (established in 1825), through its Oriental department, which translated science books in the syllabus of European schools into Urdu, paved the way for the Delhi renaissance through vernaculars[55] unlike the Calcutta renaissance through English.

That the local languages were best-suited to the fruitful dissemination of scientific knowledge was a deep-rooted conviction common among Indian intellectuals such as Raja Ram Mohan Roy, Master Ram Chandra and his contemporary Sir Syed Ahmed Khan. There was a definite political agenda underlying the translation of the best European writings into Indian languages. Sir Syed Ahmed Khan pleaded:

> Those bent on improving and bettering India must remember that the only way of compassing this is by having the whole of arts and sciences translated into their languages.[56]

The strongest argument in favour of the translation project was that the constant use of the English language by impressionable children would not only habituate them to express their thoughts in it but also 'denationalise' them. Both Master Ram Chandra and Ruchi Ram Sahni expressed their anxious concern for the alienation of the younger generation whose patriotic feelings ought to be nurtured. Both of them had actively contributed to the building of 'national character'.[57] While the former devoted his energy and talent to the translation of several European works on science in Urdu, the latter popularised information, latest inventions and various branches of scientific knowledge through his lectures in Punjabi, the most widely spoken language in this region.[58] These issues had been thrashed threadbare by the scientific society namely, Aligarh Scientific Society, Bihar Scientific Society, Indian Association for the Cultivation of Science and Punjab Science Institute. Established in the mid-nineteenth century, Sir Syed Ahmed Khan's Aligarh Scientific Society[59] and Imdad Ali's Bihar-Scientific Society[60] had similar aims, i.e. popularisation of science though regional languages, experiments with new technologies of agriculture, reformation of outdated socio-cultural customs and practices. This multi-faceted mission was carried on by Mahendra Lal Sircar's Indian Association for the Cultivation of Science (founded in 1876)[61] and Ruchi Ram Sahni's Punjab Science Institute (co-founded in 1885). All of them had prepared the ideological climate for launching the science movement in India.

Even more significant was their negotiatory strategy for creating a neutral ground for a healthy dialogue between multiple religious sensibilities of Indians and European scientific rationality. Unwilling to give up the emotional security of Hinduism, Sikhism or Islam, Indian intellectuals used science as a 'neutral terrain' or forum for mutual dialogue by redefining the nature of their respective religions through emphasis on the elements of universality and dialogic potentialities. The universalistic view of religion had been articulated by the *Dawn Society Magazine*, Calcutta, which had published a number of articles on the relationship between religion, science and technology. For example, the editorial preface to an article entitled 'Gleanings from Mohammedan Scriptures' by Mohammed Sarfaraz Hussain redefined the nature of the Indian response to the cultural hegemonisation under colonial rule. It is worthwhile to quote from it:

> When the spirit of Indian unity is in the air, it behaves us Hindus to know more and sympathise more with the thoughts and aspirations of such a large number of our fellow countrymen as follow the great prophet.[62]

Another writer Rabindra Narayan Ghosh, whose articles on scientific method and Indian culture were known for their focus on composite culture, often repudiated the colonial thesis regarding the cultural distinctiveness of Hindus and Muslims. He believed that Indian cultural traditions drew their vitality from the pragmatic concerns of the skilled workers including weavers, blacksmiths and other craftsmen. Technology and not their religious backgrounds created a common bond among them and provided the basis for the composite Hindu-Muslim culture.[63]

It may be pointed out that that the approach to the issue of relationship between religion, science and technology ranged from universalistic to exclusive depending on the historical location of a particular individual or community before the annexation of Punjab and their changing status in the course of its graduation from a non-regulation province to its integration in the empire by the British leading to consequent changes in the policies and establishment of new educational, judicial and administrative institutions.[64] However, this region continued to retain its strategic importance owing to its primacy as a recruiting ground and agrarian potential of the canal colonies.[65] More relevant in the discussion of the complex relationship between technology and religion that developed was the dominating presence and activities of the Christian missionaries, especially American Presbyterians in this region. An acute sense of alienation gripped the young Punjabis who witnessed fast-paced changes in political, legal and economic as well as educational institutions. Feeling as misfits in the colonial society and the existing Punjabi socio-cultural environment, they tried to create new values, religious vision, socio-cultural practices which would enable them live with dignity and assert their identity in the colonial space.[66]

Their rising aspirations for political, economic and cultural visibility rendered the triangular competition among the three communities extremely complex.[67] Their foremost priority was to counter the negative missionary propaganda in many forms by using the same weapons, especially print technology along with street preaching and other traditional methods. In the chapter entitled 'Technology and Religion: Recasting Hindu Consciousness Through Print in India with Special Reference to the Punjab During the Nineteenth Century', I have argued that print technology played an important role in transforming the Hindu consciousness of religion from a fuzzy awareness of sharing one god or pantheon to a belief in unity of interests whether social, political or economic on the basis of religion. It had also enabled the leadership to create a new code of conduct, social norms and unconventional set of life-cycle ceremonies. This region became the most vibrant centre for socio-cultural change including the educational movement.

NOTES

1. A few scholars have explored this relationship for example, Sandra Harding, *Is Science Multicultural? Post-colonialisms, Feminism and Epistemologies* (London: Oxford University Press, 1998); *Dhruv Raina, Images and Context: The Historiography of Science and Modernity* (Delhi: Oxford University Press, 2003); Zaheer Baber, *The Science of Empire: Scientific Knowledge, Civilization, and Colonial Rule in India* (Calcutta, Chennai, Delhi: Oxford University Press, 1998).
2. Steven Yearley, *Science, Technology and Social Change* (London: Unwin and Hymen, 1988), p. 184.
3. Joseph Needhan, *Science and Civilization in China*, 7 vols. In progress (Cambridge: Cambridge University Press, 1954). For a critical evaluation of Needham's contribution to the sociology of science, see Sal Restivo, 'Joseph Needham and the Comparative Sociology of Chinese and Modern Science', *Research in Sociology of Knowledge, Science and Art*, 1979, no. 2: pp. 25-51.
4. S. Nakayama, 'The Shifting Centres of Science', *Interdisciplinary Science Review*, Vol. 16, No. 1, 1991, pp. 82-8.
5. David Pingree, 'Hellenophilia versus the History of Science' *Iris*, Vol. 83, 1992, pp. 554-63.
6. Steven Shapin, *A Social History of Truth: Civility and Science in the Seventeenth Century England* (Chicago and London: University of Chicago, 1994).
7. Russel Dionne and Roy MacLeod, 'Science and Policy in British India, 1858-1914: Perspectives of a Persisting Belief', in S. Irfan Habib and Dhruv Raina eds, *Social History of Science in Colonial India* (Delhi: Oxford University Press, 2007), p. 160.

8. Ibid.
9. Ibid.
10. Ainslie T.Embree, *Imagining India: Essays on Indian History* (Delhi: Oxford University Press, 1989), p. 69.
11. Mathew H. Edney, *Mapping an Empire* (Chicago: University of Chicago Press, 1997), p. 2.
12. Ibid.
13. Ibid.
14. Ibid.
15. Kamlesh Mohan, 'Colonialism and Ethnic Identities in India (19th to Early 20th Century', in Ahsan Jan Qaisar and Som Prakash Verma eds; *Art and Culture: Endeavours in Interpretation* (New Delhi: Abinav Publications, 1996), p. 172. Elaborating this point, Kamlesh Mohan observes, 'During the period from 1757 to 1785, the major priority before the officials of the East India Company in Bengal was to frame an administrative system, suited for twin purposes of maintaining law and order and generating a regular income to support the administrative, military and commercial activities of the Company and to profit for the owner.... In order to perform the dual task of conquest, consolidation and control through diplomatic dealings, they had no choice but to broaden their scope of information such as knowledge of Indian political history, internal political structure of Indian states and revenue structure of rural society'.
16. Zaheer Baber, *The Science of Empire: Scientific Knowledge, Civilization, and Colonial Rule in India*, p. 144-46.
    Baber's discussion is based on J.N.I. Baker, *The History of Geography* (Oxford: Basil Blackwell, 1963) and Clement Markham, *A Memoir of Indian Surveys* (London: W.H. Allen, 1878, second edition)
17. For a detailed discussion of these projects see Bernard S. Cohn, "The Command of Language and the Language of Command", in Ranajit Guha ed., *Subaltern Studies IV, : Writings on South Asian History and Society* (New Delhi: Oxford University Press, 1994), pp. 277-329. Cohn has brought out the underlying motives of these three projects. The first project focused on the "objectification and use of Indian languages as instruments of rule". The second was a "European project, the end being to construct a history of the relationship between India and the West, to classify and order and locate their civilisations on an evaluative scale of progress and decay." The third project involved the patronage of institutions, and religious and literary

specialists who transmitted Indian traditions through a variety of media, e.g. texts, writings, recitations, paintings, sculptures, rituals and performances. Their real motive was to prove the legitimacy of their project and modes of governance by showing respect and interest in those Indians and institutions which were perceived to be active in the sustenance and transmission of tradition.

18. John Gascoigne, 'Empire' in lain MaCalman ed., *Oxford Companion to the Romantic Age* (Oxford: Oxford University Press, 1999), p. 54. Gascoigne has argued that political compulsions such as threat of foreign domination and internal political upheavals from 1765 to 1832 had forced the British to neglect their colonies.
19. Michael Foucault, "Governmentality", in G. Burchell and P. Liller eds., *The Foucault Efect: Studies in Governmentality* (London: Harvester Wheatsheaf, 1991), Cited in Zaheer Baber, *The Science of Empire*, p. 152.
20. E.J. Hobsbawm, *Nations and Nationalism Since 1780: Programme, Myth and Reality* (Cambridge: Cambridge University Press, 1991), p. 10.
21. Zaheer Baber, *n.*19, p. 153.
22. For a detailed discussion of the concept of 'hegemony' see Antonio Gramsci, *Selections from the Prison Notebooks of Gramsci*, trans and ed. Quentin Hoare and Geoffrey Nowell Smith (London: Lawrence and Wishart, 1971. For a detailed discussion of strategies of hegemony see Chapter I in this book. The term 'hegemony' was used by Gramsci to describe how the domination of one class over others is achieved by a combination of political and ideological means. Although political coercion is always important, the role of ideology in winning the consent of dominated classes may be even more significant. The balance between coercion and consent will vary from society to society, the latter being more important in capitalist societies. In Gramsci's view, the state was the chief instrument of coercive force, the winning of consent by ideological means being achieved by the institutions of civil society: the family, the religious organisations and trade unions for instance. In the case of colonial India, coercive force as well as ideological domination were used for acquiring 'hegemony'.
23. Rashmi Pant, 'The Cognitive Status of Caste in Colonial Ethnography: A Review of Some Literature on the N.W. Province and Oudh', in *Indian Economic and Social History Review*, Vol. 24, no. 2, 1987.

24. Ibid., pp. 151, 154. Pant has referred to the Census Commissioner Blunt's complaint which noted the "...difficulty of making caste lists because respondents returned names as varied as titles, surnames, the endogamous group, the occupation followed when asked to name their case". Commenting on the process, she pointed out that "it took the form of 'standardising' and 'hierarchising' caste names as a series that had an all-India applicability and were stable, as compared to local variations of caste names which were responsive to economic or political changes of status and to organised lobbying".
25. For a detailed discussion of this problem see Rajiv Kapur, *Sikh Separatism* (Delhi: Oxford University Press, 1979).
26. For more details regarding Herbert Risley's experiments in anthropometric see Ch. I in this book. Also Dilip K.Chakrabarti, *Colonial Ideology: Socio-Politics of the Indian Past* (Delhi: Munshiram Manoharlal Publishers Pvt. Ltd., 1997), pp. 116-51.
27. Resolution of Government of Bengal, Financial Department, April 30, 1885 in Financial Proceedings, March 1887, p. 36. In this resolution, a second reason was mentioned. The colonial state was keen to acquire a more minute knowledge about the Indian society in order to face the sensitive question of social reforms without hurting the sentiments of masses at large. Cited in Sekhar Bandopadhyay, 'Caste in the Perception of the Raj: A Note on the Evolution of Colonial Sociology in Bengal', *Bengal Past and Present*, 1985, Vol. civ, pts. I & II, pp. 67-8.
28. Richard Saumarez Smith, 'Rule-by-Records and Rule-by-Reports: Complementary Aspects of the British Imperial Rule of Laws', *Contributions to Indian Sociology*, Vol. 29, No. 2, p. 163.
29. Ibid., p. 156.
30. Zaheer Baber, *The Science of Empire*, p. 160.
31. For an insightful analysis of relationship between imperialist perceptions, goals and development of botanical gardens in colonial India and their instrumentality in solving the colonial problems such as Bengal famine and their role in promoting imperial trade in tea and cinchona see Ibid., pp. 160-70. For a detailed discussion of famines in colonial Bengal see Anil Chandra Banerjee, *The Agrarian System of Bengal, 1528-1793* (Calcutta: K.P. Bagchi, 1980), pp. 129-31. Also Aditi N. Chowdhuri-Zilly, *The Vagrant Peasant: Agrarian Distress and Desertion in Bengal 1770-1830* (Wiesbaden: Steiner, 1982).
32. Shiv Visvanathan, *Organizing for Science: The Making of an Industrial Laboratory* (Delhi: Oxford University Press 1985), p. 8.

According to Visvanathan, "...the institutionalisation of Western Science in India commences for all practical purposes with the establishment of the Asiatic Society of Bengal."

33. William Jones, 'The Ninth Anniversary Discourse', in *Asiatic Researches*, 1799 (1792), pp. 345-52.
34. Jones to Pitt, February 5, 1785, Letters, p. 664. Jones reported to William Pitt the Younger in February 1785 that he was almost "tempted to learn Sanskrit that I may check on the Pundits in the Court". Also Jones to Wilkins, March 1785, Ibid., p. 680. He complained to Wilkins that "it was of utmost importance that the stream of Hindu law should be pure; for we are entirely at the devotion of the native lawyers through our ignorance of Sanskrit." These two extracts explain his visit to Nadiya, a centre of Sanskrit learning, where he hoped to learn the basics of Sanskrit. A year later, he reported confidently that he was 'tolerably strong in Sanskrit' and was ready to translate a law tract by Manu, The sources mentioned above have been cited in Bernard S. Cohn, 'The Command of Language and the Language of Command', in Ranajit Guha, ed., p. 293.
35. Information regarding recruitment of Indians in the Geological Survey of India is drawn from S.N. Sen, 'The Character of the Introduction of Western Science in India during the Eighteenth and the Nineteenth Centuries' in *Indian Journal of History of Science*, Vol. I, No. 2, 1966, pp. 112-21. Col. R.H. Phillimore, *Historical Records of the Survey of India*, Vol. 2, p. 350. On the basis of records, Philmore has cited several instances of the employment of Indians who proved to be reliable and extremely useful to the surveyors. However, this practice was discouraged by the military authorities and the British government. For example, "On the advice of the military Accountant General, the Surveyor-General was informed that the employment of natives in taking surveys... is a practice which Government are by no means disposed to encourage, or to authorise any remuneration to be made for such services." Cited in Ibid.
36. Ibid.
37. Bernard S. Cohn, 'The Command of Language and the Language of Command' in Ranajit Guha ed., *Subaltern Studies IV*, p. 277.
38. Intimately linked with the requirement of public works undertaken by Lord Dalhousie as the Governor-General (1850-1856) was the goal of promoting. To promote the British government's financial interests as the supreme landlord owning the largest landed estate. Thus, technical education in India was

given more attention than in Britain.

39. Charles Grant, 'Inquiry into the Measures which Might be Adopted by Great Britain, for the Improvement of the Conditions of her Asiatic Subjects'. Reprinted in United Kingdom, *Parliamentary Papers, Report from the Select Committee on the Affairs of the East India Company, 1832*, p. 62.
40. Ibid.
41. Ibid., Minutes of Evidence Given Before the Select Committee on the Affairs of the East India Company, 1832. S. Goodfellow as quoted in the *Memoirs* of Thomas Fisher of East India House, p. 747. While defending the Bombay Engineers Institution, S. Goodfellow, Chief Engineer of Bombay Presidency, remarked on the likely impact of science on Indians, "...they can scarcely fail of relieving themselves from a load of prejudices and superstition; they will gradually, in proportion as their knowledge is spread.... become better men and better subjects."
42. Ibid.
43. Syed Mahmood, *A History of English Education: Extracts from Parliamentary Papers: Official Reports, Authoritative Despatches, Minutes and Writings of Statesmen, Resolution of the Government, etc.* (Aligarh: M.A.O. College, 1895), pp. 33-7.
44. C.A. Bayly, *Indian Society and Making of the British Empire* (Cambridge: Cambridge University Press, 1990), pp. 72-3.
45. Appointed as the Governor-General of India, William Bentinck proved to be a powerful ally of James Mill as he put some of his theories into practice. Bentinck told Mill that "I am going to British India, but I shall not be Governor-General, it is you who will be Governor-General." Cited in Javed Majeed, *Ungoverned Imaginings: James Mill's The History of British and Orientalism* (Oxford: Clarendon Press, 1992), pp.125, 128,193. For a detailed account of the influence of utilitarian theories and ideas on the British administrators and policies see Eric Stokes, *The English Unitarians and India.*
46. Cited in Syed Mahmood, *A History of English Education: Extracts from Parliamentary Papers: Official Reports, Authoritative Despatches, Minutes and Writings of Statesmen, Resolution of the Government etc.*, pp. 33,35.
47. For this extract of Charles Wood's Despatch of 1854, see J.A. Richey ed., *Selections from Educational Records 1840-1859*, p. 366.
48. Ibid., p. 365.
49. Syed Nurrullah and J.P. Naik, *A History of Education in India* (Bombay: Macmillan, 1951), p. 227.

50. Kamlesh Mohan, 'Ruchi Ram and the Pursuit of Science in a Colonial State, originally published in Narender K. Sehgal, Satpal Sangwan and Subodh Mahanti eds., *Uncharted Terrains: Essays on Science Popularisation in Pre-independence India* (New Delhi: Vigyan Prasar, 2000), p. 107.
51. S.A.I. Tirmizi, *Persian Letters of Ghalib* (New Delhi: National Archives of India, 1969), p. 50.
52. A Rahman, 'Science and Cultural Values and Historical Analysis', in *New Orient*, December 1960, Vol. I, pp. 19-20.
53. Mohammad Ismail Panipati, *Muqalai-Sir-Syed* (Lahore: n.p., 1962), Vol. I, p. 150.
54. B.N. Seal, 'Ram Mohan Roy: The Universal Man', in *Ram Mohan Roy and His Work, Centenary Publicity Booklet*, No. 1, Calcutta, June 1933, pp. 104-8.
55. Gail Minault, 'Syed Ahmed Dehlivi and the Delhi Renaissance', in R.E. Frykenberg ed., *Delhi Through the Ages* (Delhi: Oxford University Press, 1986), p. 75. Also Narayni Gupta, *Delhi between Two Empires*, p. 7. She had discussed Master Ram Chandra's contribution to the dissemination of Western Science through his paper *Fawaid-al-Nazarin*.
56. Shan Mohammad ed., *Writings and Speeches of Sir Syed Ahmed Khan* (Bombay: Asia Publishing House, 1972), pp. 231-2.
57. For a detailed discussion on this issue see Ruchi Ram Sahni, 'Self-Revelations of an Octogenarian' (Manuscript is lying with his grandson Professor Ashok Sahni, Panjab University, Chandigarh). Both Munshi Zakaullah, a student of Master Ram Chandra and Akshay Kumar Dutt had shown acute awareness of and concern with the consequences of English education, especially its role in alienating young impressionable students from their own national culture.
58. Ibid., pp. 256-7.
59. For a detailed discussion on Aligarh Scientific Society see S. Irfan Habib, 'Promoting Science and its World-View in the Mid-Nineteenth Century India', in Deepak Kumar ed., *Science and Empire: Essays in Indian Context (1700-1947)*, (Delhi: Anamika Prakashan for NISTAD, 1991), pp. 141-6.
60. Ibid., pp. 146-7.
61. For a detailed discussion on Indian Association for the Cultivation of Science see Chittabrata Palit, 'Mahendra Lal Sircar 1833-1904: The Quest for National Science', in Ibid., pp. 154-9.
62. *The Dawn* (Calcutta), December 1902, p. 176. Cited in Irfan Habib and Dhruv Raina eds., *Social History of Science in Colonial India*,

pp. 238-9.

63. Rabindra Narayan Ghosh, 'The Civilisation of the Northern India: A Contribution to the Study of the Hindu-Muslim Relations', in Ibid, May 1911, pp. 84-70.
64. For a discussion of policies in the British Punjab see Imran Ali, *The Punjab under Imperialism, 1885-1947* (Delhi: Oxford University Press, 1989). Also Kamlesh Mohan, 'The Colonial State, Agrarian Policy and Peasant Response in the Punjab during the Nineteenth century', in the *Pakistan Journal of History and Culture,* Vol. XI, No. I (January-June 1994).
65. Tan Tai Yong, *The Garrison State: The Military, Government and Society in Colonial Punjab 1849-1947* (New Delhi, London: Sage Publications, 2005).
66. For a discussion of policies in the British Punjab see Imran Ali , *The Punjab under Imperialism, 1885-1947* (Delhi: Oxford University, Press, 1989) Also Kamlesh Mohan, 'The Colonial State, Agrarian Policy and Peasant Response in the Punjab during the Nineteenth Century', in the *Pakistan Journal of History and Culture,* Vol. xv.
67. Kenneth W. Jones, *Arya Dharm: Hindu Consciousness in Nineteenth Century Punjab* (New Delhi: Manohar Book Service, 1976), pp. 8-13. Also Shyamala Bhatia, *Social Change and Politics in Punjab 1898-1910* (New Delhi: Enkay Publishers Pvt. Ltd., 1987), pp. 114-23.

1

The Colonial Ethnography

Imperial Pursuit of Knowledge for Hegemony in British India (Late Nineteenth to Early Twentieth Century)

The colonial ethnography was crafted as an essential constituent as well as the tool of the legitimising discourse of the imperial Indian state from mid-nineteenth century onwards. With the epistemological shift from religion to science, the colonial administrators and policy-makers as interpreters and practitioners of the European rationalist discourse had given a new angle to the study and representation of the 'other' in Africa and Asia whom they were to 'subdue, administer, convert and improve without halting and without question'.[1] While establishing rationalist connection between precise knowledge and social control, they were to give statistical content to the 'imagined communities' in B. Anderson's[2] phrase. To control the Indian society without the use of naked brutal force, i.e. to arrange its acaquiescence or 'hegemony', it was essential to locate it in taxonomic systems. With an eye on this long-term politico-economic objective of the multiple subjugation of India, the colonial state initiated the cumbersome process of counting through ethnographic surveys, census maps and statistical data for constructing and pigeonholing Indians into primordial identities and racial typologies by manipulating scientific theories and methods.

The major argument in this paper is that the initiation and formalization of the colonial ethnography in British India from the 1860s to the 1930s, apart from deflecting the Indological discourse from Orientalism to 'scientific racism', had played a crucial role in the consolidation of imperial 'hegemony' and the identity-formation of Indians on the twin-basis of religion and caste. Undoubtedly, the intervention of the colonial administrators-turned-ethnograpahers such as James Wise, Herbert Risley, E. Thurston, Denzil Ibbetson, J.H. Hutton and L.S.S. O'Malley was decisive in the process of manufacturing and freezing identities of individuals and communities.

I would like to draw attention to the other side of my argument. The colonial subjects did not accept the negative image of 'self' and their civilisation stoically. They refused to be preserved as exhibits in imperial museums and be treated as passive receptacles of anthropological debates, official reconstructions and conceptualisations of Indian society, history and cultural traditions. I have discussed the response of Indian society in a separate paper.*

It may be pointed out that a detailed analysis of 'religion' as a reference-point for identity does not fall within the scope of this paper which primarily focuses on the interplay between imperial pursuit of knowledge, hegemony and colonial identities.

The paper is divided into four sections: I. Construction of the Colonial State and Its Strategies for Hegemony; II. Imperial Discourse on Race and the Indian People : Physical Types in India; III. Caste Identities in Colonial Ethnography; IV. Conclusion.

---

* Kamlesh Mohan, 'Constructing Religion and Caste and Manipulating Identities' *Social Sciences Research Journal* (March-July 1992), I, 1-2, 139-176.

I

Construction of the Colonial State and Its Strategies for Hegemony

Construction of the Colonial State

In this section, my intention is to highlight the centrality of knowledge in the colonial discourse which was conducted through two related processes: construction of the colonial state and formulation of its strategies for hegemony, i.e. a consensual basis for political control with occasional resort to force disciplining the recalcitrant and ignorant people. As a legacy from the European rationalism, the aphorism 'Knowledge is Power' had acquired a double connotation with the expanding British empire in Africa and India. In the first sense, it implied the acquisition of knowledge through scientific tools and methods about the mentalities, internal organisation of Indian society, its politico-economic power-networks and about the idiom of the civilisational discourse of its people. In the second sense, its emphasis was on the dissemination of Western education in order to enable the colonial people to internalise imperialist perceptions of Indian history and its positive projections of the colonial state and its policies. Briefly, it can be termed as the colonisation of consciousness.

A brief explication of the process of the construction of the colonial state is relevant because it provided the mediating structures for articulating the shifts and priorities in the imperial projects and ideology. Its relevance is further stressed by the fact of its being the surrogate of the Crown from the mid-nineteenth century onwards, i.e. the executive and legislative arm for political and social control of the colonies. Central to the ideological dimension of imperialism in the second half of the nineteenth century was the heightened consciousness of ethical superiority, political and scientific fitness of the Anglo-Saxon race to carry out its civilising mission holding 'Whiteman's burden' on their heart, guns in their hands and God on their side.

The colonial state underwent the process of construction in the literal sense.[3] It passed through two stages and did not grow out of the internal logic of the pre-British Indian society and the state to which it was a successor. The view that the Battle of Plassey laid the foundation of the British empire is very simplistic. The actual process of imperialist expansion from 1765 to 1818 and the transformation of commercial privileges of a trading company into a political power was slow and far more complex. At one level, it can be explained in terms of the structures of production systems but its applicability depends upon the degree of importance attached to economic forces in a particular society. At another level, this process may be interpreted from the socio-cultural angle, i.e. the discussion about the encounter of two different civilisational discourses, two epistemologies and two different principles of construction of society and state. A combination of these two approaches is more helpful for analysis.

At the first stage of the construction of the political structure, i.e. 1798 to 1818, the Company had performed the basic function of collection of land revenue and tribute within the framework of the Mughal classification for revenue and tenurial system. Their administration had sought to assume powers of a centralised political system which resembled the feudal absolutist state of Western Europe. Its major duties were to introduce a uniform legal system and communication system, consolidation of private property and abolition of internal barriers to trade. The principle of legal equality was theoretically upheld when Cornwallis claimed that the state itself would be subject to the rule of law from 1793 onwards. However, the task of the codification of Indian public law was not completed until the 1860s. Gradually, Indian society submitted to the imperial authority, its law and codes which regulated social relations, property ownership, eviction suits and exchange relations. But the people had not yet accepted the intellectual and moral leadership of their colonial masters.

The second stage in the construction of the colonial state came in the second half of the nineteenth century when the British political power was well-entrenched and the Indian experience of the 1857 revolt had reduced the possibility of the regrouping of the old ruling classes as a rival centre of power.

It had coincided with the second stage of the colonial exploitation and polarisation of the developing industrial and commercial interests. Pressurised by their lobbying, the metropolitan government had underlined the need for the transformation of indigenous structures in order to equip India to serve as a market for goods and a supplier of raw materials. It could not be done without destroying India's early advantage in textile production and trade as well as indigenous technology. This was how the British spokesmen of European rationalism had manipulated the argument to wipe out Indian technology and appropriated its epistemological space.

It was in this climate of ideological fermentation, dominated by the consciousness of scientific and technological ascendancy, that the liberals and the 'radical' democrats in England hammered the framework within which the imposing structure of the colonial state was to be further elaborated and altered in design. The most crucial development, which determined the shape of the colonial state in India in the second phase, was the transfer of the political control of India from the hands of the Company to the British Parliament. Based on the principle of creating checks and balances, the gradually evolving colonial state was made accountable to the British people.

It can be said that the period falling roughly between 1833 and the end of the nineteenth century was the period when essential features and tendencies were being evolved that went into the construction of a specific type of colonial state in India. Once India was subordinated to the British Parliament, the evolution of this state could not but be influenced by the ideas and political tendencies prevalent in British society. Henceforth, the colonial state became the site for contest between liberalism, growing powerful since 1818, and already existing approach of conservatism. In spite of the clash between the farsighted liberal experiment and unimaginative conservative adventure[4], a compromise formula gradually emerged on the understanding that they were serving the same goal – the maintenance of control over India. Thus, rationalism, the ideological plank of 'advanced' European nations, had led to a truce between the two contending approaches.

The further development of the colonial state was determined by the state of relationship between the 'authoritarian principles' and 'liberal principles'—clash or compromise. On the contentious issues of free press, self-government and dissemination of Western education, especially science education in India, the conservatives and the liberals martialled their forces under two banners 'progress' and 'repression', thus emphasising their fundamental differences of outlook. While Lord Ripon had chosen the former, Lord Lytton had espoused the latter line.[5]

By the last decade of the nineteenth century, the task of constructing the colonial state had reached a final stage as its essential principles and agencies such as legislative, judiciary and executive had become operative in a big way.

Strategies for Hegemony

Once the colonial state established itself, it faced the problem of securing social control or arranging acquiescence of the subject people and formulating constructs and strategies for an intelligible hegemonic discourse. In other words, how the British raj was to contrive arguments and prepare the mental climate for the ideological rationalisation of the endless perpetuation of the colonial rule. The first logical step in this direction was to fit its colonial policy within the framework of the British political discourse in the metropolis. Being the extended arm of the British Crown, the colonial state was accountable to the British people who were likely to evaluate imperial attitudes and actions on significant issues in Indian politics by the criteria of justice, effectiveness and honour, accepted as ground rules in internal politics in Britain.[6]

The hegemonic discourse as well as its strategies, like the colonial state was the product of European rationalist theory,[7] which attached great importance to technical knowledge as an instrument of control, conquest and imaging invincibility. Undoubtedly, the colonial state was far more powerful than the metropolitan government whose use of open force was limited by the democratic rules and competing ideological pressures of liberal and conservative forces in British domestic politics. The colonial state's functionaries had also to keep in mind the fact of publicity of their actions and the consequences of hallucinations of invincibility that go with despotic power. Clive and Hastings, who had succumbed to the temptation of illegal gratification, were punished for transgressing the ground rules of conduct for holding public office.

Turning to the strategies for legitimising the presence of the colonial state, its authority and economic exploitation, two alternatives seemed suited to the political situation in India. The first one required the new rulers to adopt the political structure as well as the cultural discourse of the existing Mughal regime. The second strategy stipulated that the structure and discourse of Indian polity and society be remodelled through a serious missionary effort for the spread of Western education.[8] The colonial state used both these strategies alternately or a judicious mix of both depending on the state of its political well-being and authority. While laying the terrain of its discourse and terms of reference for the guidance and comprehension of their sympathisers among the colonial elite, it avoided rigidity for pragmatic reasons.

In the early stages of the Company rule the British rulers had chosen the first strategy. It was evident from the adoption of traditional nomenclatures such as *diwani* or *sarkar* as well as cultural and symbolic order. It was safe for the colonial state, which had not possessed real political authority and economic power, to enforce social reforms to restructure social relations and manufacture identities.

Despite the Company government's broad conformity with the authoritarian structure of Mughal administration and its paternal character, a gradual instrusion of British concepts was clearly noticed. Instead of borrowing this and that from India for their own political structure, the British, according to Percival Spear, " ....took over the Indian state and then made additions and adjustments according to their own ideas".

However, quite a few Company functionaries, at least upto the early nineteenth century, were convinced of the necessity of legitimising their authority, particularly the revenue system on the basis of a thorough knowledge and record of interlocking rights, customs and obligations of the village community. Thomas Munro, Charles Metcalf and Mountstuart Elphinstone's respective discovery of the peasant proprietor, community of cultivating *zamindars* and controlling *muqaddams*[10] was as much a product of their long residence, laborious surveys and close contact with the village life and its institutions as of the rulers' obligation or compulsion to hammer a more remunerative revenue system for the lands seized from Tipu Sultan, the Nawab of Oudh and the Maratha *Peshwa*.

By the mid-nineteenth century when the British political authority was not plagued by any rivals and threats, the rulers abandoned their majestic aloofness and compromising and beseeching tone. Apart from constructing their own judicial set up including law and codes and legislative and executive institutions, the British potentates were seriously engaged in creating colonial consciousness. Henceforth, their new allies, i.e. the middle classes of Calcutta and not the traditional rulers seemed more trustworthy as targets of enculturation and suitable receptacles for their racist vision of the non-Western world and notions of biological determinism until they learnt to turn the hegemonic discourse against their colonial masters.

In accordance with the second strategy, the colonial programme for the spread of Western education (with special focus on scientific knowledge generated in Europe) was intensified. It had two objectives: utilitarian and ideological. For its utilitarian purpose, the colonial state was to train an army of English-knowing Indians who would fill in the lower rungs of various administrative departments and that too on meagre pay.

Its second purpose but its main premise underlying the introduction of English education in India was to conciliate the people and prepare them for the new British East India Company regime[11] which had won its supremacy with the help of arms. Macaulay and many of his contemporaries believed that military conquest had only won them a 'precarious hegemony'. The most enduring and the most profitable conquest was the one over mind.[12] In order to mould India into a replica of England—the best model of social, political and material progress—and to serve the needs of industrial England, moral mission or civilisational mission in India, through the dissemination of Western education, was given utmost importance.

The first generation of Indian intelligentsia in nineteenth century Bengal had eagerly assimilated this ideological perspective. It was a case of instant success for the colonial mission as it had inspired a belief that it was only through the medium of English education that the reservoir of European scientific knowledge would be opened to them. Raja Ram Mohan Roy, who like his contemporaries regarded Britain as the 'chosen instrument' for leading India to the path of political and economic modernisation, had adopted an idealised view of the state without making any distinction between the objectives and functions of an alien and native government.[13] In his view, financial investment by selected Europeans as settlers in India would bring capital and technology – the preconditions for the industrialisation of a poor and backward country.[14]

Obviously, the rhetoric of rationalism which had projected the progressive characteristics of the Western, especially British society, such as egalitarianism, scientific knowledge and democratic political institutions and economic development, had a powerful attraction for the 'Young Bengal' group and other college students of Calcutta. Equipped with theoretical tools, resources and techniques, these urban English-educated students rejected their own social traditions and past in the hope of being accepted as equal participants in the colonial-rationalist dialogue. Ironically, the Bengali *babu's* efforts enabled him to acquire remarkable knowledge of European history with sympathy but a negative and second hand Euro-centric view of Indian history and civilisation.[15] This moment of triumph for the hegenomic discourse had two grave implications for the colonial elite. Firstly, they were weighed down by an inferiority complex and secondly, by a feeling of alienation from their ideological cultural moorings. In the long run, it bred disillusionment and contradictions between the colonised and the colonial power.

Along with the extensive drive for Western education, the British rulers carried on their discourse through another effective and unusual project–refiguring and restructuring of society. As practitioners of the enlightenment theory of knowledge, the British civil servants began a scientific exercise of enumerating and classifying Indians. The underlying belief was that control of society depended upon precise knowledge of its composition and location of its members in the taxonomic system.[16] In order to obtain a clear picture of the society which they were to rule perpetually according to their perception, the colonial administrator-turned-ethnographer began the comprehensive and time-consuming process of counting through census maps, statistical tables and pigeonholing and classifying people into races, tribes and castes. The colonised Indians would gradually become skilful in counting and use their weight as 'enumerated' communities to extract political concessions from the colonial government. Thus, the scientific process of enumeration became an instrument in the hands of the British rulers to keep Indians divided along caste and community lines and carve an interventionist role for the colonial state.

The idea, that the British would not only choose their opponents but also predetermine the path that they would follow by consciously preempting development along one path preferably reform rather than revolution, was the product of the rationalist thinking of Charles E. Trevelyan.[17] It was within the framework inspired by this idea that the British policy makers were designing their tactical moves for the constitutional development of India.

The European rationalist belief in the superiority of Western knowledge, Western civilisation and nations bred intolerance of other cultures and epistemologies. Lord Macaulary had projected the cultural chauvinism of the British people particularly of rulers in his famous *Minute* (1835).

> The intrinsic superiority of Western literature is indeed fully admitted. ...I have never found one amongst them (Orientalists) who could deny that a single shelf of a good European library was worth the whole native literature of India and Arabia.[18]

Later, he demanded that no artificial encouragement should be given at all to 'absurd history, absurd metaphysics, absurd theology.'

Thus, the orientalists' faith in the aphorism 'knowledge is power' was integrated into the legitimisation discourse of the colonial state from the 1860s onwards. With the convergence of the high tide in industrial capitalism and bourgeois imperialism in Britain, the wide-eyed curiosity of the early Orientalists had been transformed into the pursuit of 'scientific and historical goals'. In fact, the period between the 1860s to the 1930s witnessed the growth of a closer connection between science, colonialism, imperialism and racism. When modern science aligned itself with imperialism, it lost its spirit of accommodation and respect for 'separate, often interacting epistemologies in history'.[19] Consequently, it began to claim a monopoly in knowledge in order to retain its claimed superiority. This monopoly was based on the premise that all other forms of acquisition or accumulation of knowledge, all other epistemologies, are worthless, antiquated, magical and must be eliminated".

Interestingly, the scientific method itself was used as a coloniser.[20] A novel argument for the legitimation of colonialism – the aggressive outer arm of capitalism – was incorporated in the discourse of enlightenment which celebrated and linked scientific genius with the Anglo-Saxon race. For example, Joshia wrote in 1885:

> Only those races which have produced machinery seemed capable of using it with best results. Those races which, like the African and the Malay, are many centuries behind the Anglo-Saxon in development, seem as incapable of operating complicated machinery as they are of adopting and successfully administering representative government.[21]

This justification of imperialism and expansionism into Africa and Asia was based on the same ideology that had enabled English immigrants to the United States to hunt, displace, and exterminate millions of American-Indians. The argument about the limits of diffusion and scientific capabilities of the colonial people, while establishing the superiority of the Anglo-Saxon race as an imperial breed, also put forth the case for perpetual domination.[22]

This argument was used later on to justify resource extraction from the colonies. On the basis of the law of entropy, the second law of thermodynamics, the colonial state argued that the right to own land and forests should be determined by political and 'scientific fitness'. The expropriation of redefinition of 'use-rights' of the villages and tribals created a deep sense of injustice. While the villagers, who regarded the surrounding forests as their own, were unwilling to treat the cutting of trees as a crime, the British officials saw the traditional practices as totally inconsistent with the logic of conservation and general 'principle of property'. Thus, forest settlement operations and laws became the site of contest between the people and the colonial state.[23]

II

Imperial Discourse on Race and the Indian People: Physical Types in India

Imperial Discourse on Race

In this section, I shall discuss how far the representation of the Indian people in terms of racial typologising was influenced by the drastic shift in the European intellectual paradigm, i.e. from ethnocentric to 'scientific racism' in the wake of path breaking achievements in science and technology. The twin experience of imperial expansion and industrialisation, leading to class conflict in Britain, had also shaped their racial attitudes. The important issue to be raised is whether the arguments and strategies for legitimising the presence of the colonial state and the perpetuation of imperial authority in Asia and Africa shared a common ground with the discourse on race.

The discourse on race refers to the content of images, beliefs and evaluations of the colonised people whether in Africa or India. The British perception of the 'other' as the inferior biological species was a continuing legacy of slave plantocracy in the colonies of West Indies, especially Barbados and was woven into its later social thought and intellectual tradition and colonial practice. The 'golden age' of the British empire from the 1830s to its decline in the 1940s, witnessed a growth of interest in the study of visually different races, accompanied by a variety of 'scientific racism' based on social Darwinist and eugenic notions of white racial fitness. Being an intellectual elaboration of a deep-rooted curiousity about 'exotic' cultures such as those of the Middle East, and the Far East, subsumed under 'orientalism', the study of man and society became linked with physical anthropology. It applied scientific theories and tools for racial typologising of the 'other' in order to hierarchise them as inferior varieties of human species.

The modern ideas of 'race' and manifestation of 'racism' as it is known today, are European in origin, deeply rooted in history, institutions, belief systems and in the folk-ways of the European peoples. These were universalised and spread to all parts of world through European colonial expansion. The spread of European racism was facilitated because of the superior technology, particularly, faster means of global communication and acquisition of economic and political power by the European people at a particular period and peculiarities of capitalist development. Its spread was further aided by the principal agents of colonialism and imperialism particularly merchants, Christian missionaries, settlers and officials.

As a result of the secularisation of culture and the growth of increasing dominance and hegemony of science in the nineteenth century, a major change had occurred in the European representations of the 'other'.[24] This change had signified the formulation of a discourse of race which may be called biological determinism or 'scientific racism'. This discourse of race, largely a product of the misapplication of scientific principles, especially the evolutionary theory, was reproduced throughout Europe, North America and their colonies in Africa and Asia.

A wide circulation of racist images, beliefs and evaluations was facilitated by the scientists who contributed to this debate, shared their formulations and evaluated each others' writings. For example, writings of the British theorists Lord Kanes and Charles White were reviewed by Stanhope Smith in a book *Essay on the Causes of the Variety of Complexion and Figure in the Human Species* (1787). The science of phrenology was pioneered by Franz Joseph Gall and Johan Gaspar Spurzheim in Germany and was developed by George Combe in Scotland. Through this process of exchange of ideas, phrenology found space in *Crania Americana* in 1839 and *Crania Aegyptiaca* in 1844, when George Combe discussed it with his American friend.

The cephalic index, invented by Anders Retzius in Sweden, inspired a significant portion of the work of Paul Broca in Paris. The work of colonial ethnographers namely, Herbert Risley, had constructed and elaborated racial typologies to classify Indian people by an extensive use of cephalic and nasal indices. A very significant product of collaborative effort was the book entitled *Types of Mankind* (1854) and it remained a major influence on the theory of 'race' for the next few decades which saw at least its nine editions.

One of its authors, Louis Agassiz, was a Swiss naturalist, who had been influenced by the French economist George Curier and migrated to the United States in 1846 where he collaborated with Joshia Nott and George Giddon. Thus, the development and elaboration of the discourse of race had been facilitated by international effort and enterprise.[25]

However, England became the important centre for the intellectual elaboration of 'scientific racism' which can be defined as :

> ... the creation and employment of a body of legitimately scientific or patently psuedo-scientific data as rationales for the preservation of poverty, inequality of opportunity for upward mobility and related regressive social arrangements.[26]

In the course of its implementation, 'scientific racism' has often institutionalised and lent scientific respectability to racist dogma and practices that were all far older than science itself.

Three historical developments combined to make England the logical site on which 'scientific racism' was to be born. While the agricultural revolution had also occurred in other European countries under the lead of England, the Georgian Enclosure Acts were confined to England only. Between the period from

1750 to 1800 when the prospects of profitability of large scale agriculture became real, the Georgian Enclosure Acts were legislated. As a result, thousands of rural English families were legally evicted and denied use of common lands and subjected to harsh changes, dislocations and forced to live on private and parish charity. Secondly, for all its long range economic gains for the nation and alternative means of livelihood for the landless poor, the industrial revolution had increased the rate of infant mortality for their children who spent lives in poverty and the pollution-choked, grimy new factories and coal towns. Thomas Malthus (1766-1834), the first Professor of Political Economy at Haileybury and the author of *An Essay on the Principle of Population* (1798), opposed all social measures including legislation for the improvement of individual family and public health on the plea of 'laws of nature'. As the progenitor of the first major theory of human inferiority of the lower and middling classes, presented in the language of science, Malthus had paved the way for the less theological and more mathematical systems of 'scientific racism', propagated from Galton and Gobineau to Lapouge and Davenport. Malthus's thesis, which combined 'scripture with science, theology with mathematics, and heavenly revelation with political economy', was a transitional posture in the development of the discourse on race.[27]

Malthus' thesis of 'laws of nature' became a basis for the three independent discoveries of the idea of progressive evolution resulting from the struggle for survival—Herbert Spencer, Charles Darwin and Alfred R. Wallace in 1852, 1858 and 1855 respectively. However, it was Spencer who introduced the phrase 'survival of the fittest' in his *Principles of Biology* (1864, 1866) and he pioneered the cult of social Darwinism. This bio-cultural theory served as a perfect rationalisation for imperial conquest and control.

Indian People: Physical Types

The colonial ethnologist-cum-ethnographer, while functioning as the cognitive eye of the British rulers, had transposed the anthropological debate from the metropolis to the periphery.

W. Crooke and H.H. Risley, who were leading colonial ethnographers, frankly acknowledged their debt to European anthropology. After a prolonged and serious consultation with the professional organisations of anthropologists in Britain and in accordance with the guidelines framed by them, Risley had organised ethnological experiments and ethnographic and census surveys in India. In these anthropological investigations, the major reference points were race, caste and religion.

Fully convinced of the visible benefits of application of scientific concepts, principles and techniques in constructing a coherent picture of modern Britain, the professional anthropologists and colonial administrators-turned-ethnographers tried to link their discipline with colonial practice. This is a partial explanation of their growing interest in undertaking ethnological studies, social surveys and compiling multi-purpose statistical information on Indian society. By an application of the scientific method for studying colonial subjects in their social and ecological environment, they hoped to generate knowledge about their physical and mental characteristics, behavioural patterns, social customs, internal organisation of various communities and their economic activities for use in the formulation of policies, legislation and above all for political control. In fact, statistical and social surveys had provided the groundwork on which the early policies of the East India Company were based. For example, Colonial Secretary William Henry Sykes, a founder member of the London Statistical Society and the Statistical Reporter to the Government of Bombay in the 1820s, contributed many papers on India to the British Society for the Advancement of Science.[28] These quantitative surveys and ethnological studies had been inspired by a racist world-view which was tied to the British self-image of a master race—'vigorous, industrious and intrepid',[29] and a society which epitomised the highest stage of development. The official perception of Indian society was articulated by the Commissioner for the Census of the Lower Provinces of Bengal 1855 when he observed that the country was not ready for the '... existence of those free institutions which a higher civilisation demands.'[30] This position of the colonial state was an endorsement of the views of the spokesmen of imperial ideology namely, Henry Maine. Believing in the paradigm of 'backward' and 'advanced' races and societies, he argued that India might progress under British guidance as Germany had done under Rome.[31]

After his appointment as the Law Member of the Governor-General's Council in 1862, Maine bluntly stated his view of the Indian society and the imperial role when he remarked how the 'English race prevented the flood of barbarism' and the empire had the 'duty to rebuild upon its own principles that which it destroys.'[32] In other words, he had firmly located race in the colonial discourse.

Similar justifications of the colonial presence and its 'civilisation mission' in the colonies came from the Government of India itself which found it difficult to sustain the eighteenth century myth of an 'undifferentiated orient with rectilinear simplicity of social structures.'[33] It clearly stated the necessity of studying the social customs and manners of the Indian subjects because this knowledge furnished the key to political control.

Motivated by the new taxonomic trend in the European intellectual tradition, the colonial state instructed its officials to undertake statistical surveys and produce discursive accounts concerning social units of race, tribe and caste, religion and popular customs, economic activity and land tenure systems in the territories brought under the British rule throughout the nineteenth century.

The early ethnographic and cadastral surveys owed to the initiative and enterprise of individuals. In proportion with the growing clarity in the conceptualisation of the hegemonic discourse, these surveys and ethnographic accounts became more comprehensive, systematic and a well-coordinated official enterprise. The best examples of this kind of administrative literature were produced by the labours of Wilson, Dalton, Ibbetson, Risley, Hutton and many others. They had given an empirical content to the abstract notions[34], earlier popularised by travelogues, missionary writings and selective Orientalist constructions of Indian religion, language and history.

The British evinced special concern with the question of race, religion and caste. For example, in the period leading upto the 1871-82 census, the Sub-Committee to the Statistical Committee on the proposed census forms, attempted to define these terms. In the case of race it noted :

> It is impossible to enter race and caste together. For instance, a Sonthal or a Cole may be Mussulman or a Native Christian. If we merely enter him as a Native Christian we lose his race; if we merely designate him as a Sonthal the fact of his being Native Christian or Mussulman escapes notice.[35]

Their serious concern for devising the physical and socio-cultural categories (perceived as correct in their view for classifying the subject people) was also underpinned by the imperial compulsion to standardise and centralise the process, so that Indian society could be viewed as a whole and, indeed compared with other societies especially the progressive Western societies. It was reflected in the growing interest in scientific, ethnological and ethnographic studies in the colonies. The recommendation of the British Association for the advancement of Science, for incorporating such data in the ensuing Indian Census 1901, was self-evident. While accepting this proposal, the Government of India emphasised its importance in its letter to the Secretary of State for India. The letter read, 'India is a vast storehouse of social and physical data which only need be recorded in order to contribute to the solution of the problems which are being approached in Europe'.[36] This was the official argument for the incorporation of a comprehensive section on Indian social structure in the Indian Census 1901. This ethnographic trend was amended and further developed in subsequent census reports and separate statistical volumes. Herbert Risley, who had conducted a detailed investigation into the customs of castes and tribes of Bengal as a Special Officer for the whole of Bengal (took charge on January 28, 1885), made a substantial contribution in constructing the social morphology of this region.

Risley had also systematically developed the ethnological line of enquiry from the 1880s onwards, which had earlier been confined to the stray efforts, through census operations for settlement of revenue and other purposes. Already grappling with the issue of the origins of intermediate and lower castes, he used this opportunity to locate and explicate the social process of the 'gradual Brahmanisation of the aboriginal non-Aryan, or casteless tribes', mentioned by Alfred Lyall. Excited by the anthropometric experiments to solve the problem of the racial basis of nationality in England, he turned to the :

> ... possibility of applying to the leading tribes and castes of Bengal, the methods of recording and comparing typical physical characteristics which have yielded valuable physical results in other parts of the world.[37]

The positive response from W.H. Flower, the then Director of the Natural History Department in the British Museum, and his advice to Risley to study Paul Topinard's works, urged the latter to draft his scheme for anthropometry for tribes of Bengal. A close perusal of *Elements d' Anthropologie* (1855) enthused Risley so much that he placed an order for Dr. Topinard's "anthropometric box" containing four simple instruments. In late February 1886, he received the box and made some experiments on the *Rajbansis* of Rangpur without facing any difficulty.

In March 1886, Risley's proposal to supplement the enquiries by an examination of the physical characteristics of selected castes and tribes was immediately sanctioned by the Government of India, it was extended to the North-Western Provinces, Punjab and the Central Provinces. On the ground of providing a comparative dimension to Risley's experiments and 'probable value' of the result of his investigations, the Imperial Government gave him an extension of his tenure as a Special Officer upto March 31, 1988.

Later on, Risley sent his whole scheme to some leading anthropologists and Indologists in Europe namely, Francis Galton, Sir John Lubbock, Professor Max Mueller, Professor Topinard and Sir Henry Maine. All of them expressed their satisfaction with the procedure of investigation, conducted with the help of approved scientific methods. Earlier, W.H. Flower had also endorsed the value of physical examination as a source of data for ethnology. Information from language and customs could be helpful in a limited way as these were likely to be misleading.[38] It is obvious that a large number of European scholars held similar views on establishing the racial inferiority of Indians with the help of so-called scientific methods.

After years of relentless labour, Risley completed *The Tribes and Castes of Bengal* which ran into four volumes. The first two volumes which came out in print in 1891, contained the 'Ethnographic Glossary', while the next two contained the anthropometric data. Thus, the new trend of Indian ethnography was formalised and it led to the growth of voluminous literature in the next three decades. It reached its culmination in J.H. Hutton's Indian census, 1931.

As for the administrative value of the ethnological part of his *magnum opus* was concerned, Risley himself conceded '...it will be of little or no use for administrative purposes, and in fact will interest only a small number of persons in India and Europe.'[39] It is not the whole truth. Believing that the application of the anthropometric method would 'detach considerable masses of non-Aryans from the general body of Hindus',[40] he instructed the enumerators to exclude those persons with black complexion, and very broad and depressed noses from the list of high castes. Similarly, men of very fair complexion with sharp noses should be rejected because there was the possibility of miscegenation. Working on Alfred Lyall's theory of the bi-racial composition of Hindu society—the higher castes belonging to the Aryan and lower to the Dravidian stock—he hoped to delineate the ethnic composition of the majority community.[41] In his view, this knowledge would be of 'political value' for the colonial state which was trying to identify the 'depressed underclass' for the segmentation of the nationalist forces.

The colonial administrators, who had been instrumental in developing the strategies of hegemonic discourse and construction of social morphology of India, were divided on the validity of anthropometric data. For example, E.A. Gait, while endorsing Risley's view that 'caste largely corresponds to race', had drawn attention to the diametrically opposite results of physical measurements by other ethnologists namely, W. Crooke in the United Provinces, R.E. Enthoven in Bombay and E. Thurston in Madras. O'Donnel has argued that even the Bengal measurements were often at variance.[42]

Barring the controversy about the viability of anthropometric methods for determining the racial composition[43] of Indian society, the colonial ethnographers had formulated some common assumptions about its nature. From the mid-nineteenth century onwards, most of the British ethnological, historical and sociological accounts had used pluralistic theories to delineate Indian society. In their view, it consisted of an endless series of culturally distinct communities, demarcated along lines of castes, religion and community. One basic assumption guiding their analysis was about its bi-racial composition: Aryan and Dravidians. Dr. Caldwell, for example, saw the South Indian Brahmin-non-Brahmin divide as the product of Aryan (Brahmin) conquest and subordination of the Dravidian (non-Brahmin) peoples. Risley, Alfred Lyall and L.S.S. O'Malley had applied this theory for explaining the spread of Hindu religion among the tribal communities.

In colonial ethnography, this concept of bi-polarity has been used to project the separateness between Hindus and Muslims. On the basis of the multiple criteria of race, religion and culture, they argued that Indian society was permanently divided into two major religious communities: the Hindus and Muslims, having two separate legal codes and two distinct social and cultural traditions. Therefore, their differences were irreconciliable.[41] It is not accidental that Hindus had been defined in terms of their racial characteristics and demarcated as primordial social groups, fixed in status or ranks on the basis of *varna,* purity-impurity criteria and marriage customs. However, this ethnological description of Hindu society could not be of much use for the formulation of administrative decisions and state policies unless supplemented by precise knowledge about their numerical position and statistical data about their socio-economic conditions. This object was to be secured through the use of quasimathematical methods in the decennial census, discussed in Section III.

The British ethnological writings have also endorsed the concept of race-stratification. These various racial segments, it was argued, were capable of being ranked on the basis of their inherent attributes. For example, the 'martial' races of the Rajputs and Muslims of the North were seen to hold their premier positions in rural society by right of blood and ancestry which gave them their special martial qualities. Owing to their utility as soliders, they received special economic privileges and protection from the *raj.* The "criminal" tribes of South India, who were perceived to be inherently deviant and recalcitrant, suffered from increasing restrictions on their civil liberties through law.[44] Besides, 'commercial races' and 'agricultural races' also figured on the list of 'Tribes', circulated for collecting information on 'specimens of interest', i.e. races in India.[45] The colonial perception of Indian society was evidently grounded in systems of reckoning and evaluation whose reference points were mainly ethnicity and race. Thus, construction of racial typologies had partially unravelled the mysteries of a bewildering complex constituted by a population of at least forty millions of many races and creeds, representing interests so important and varied'.[46]

III

Caste Identities in Colonial Ethnography

The main focus of discussion in this section is colonial ethnographic thinking, especially, its locale where information about caste was collected, classified, cross-tabulated, compared and presented. Detailed information about caste-structure and its distribution at district, provincial and all-India levels was collected with a view to reveal the essential attributes and vulnerability of each of the groups. As these census reports, social surveys, ethnogrophical accounts, caste-index volumes and cadastral surveys generated information about land, health, disease, climate, occupation, religion and social-structure for official use, it can be inferred that colonial ethnography was used as an instrument for the formulation of an imperial strategy to understand and master the use of keys for social control.

The empiricist studies of Bengal, Punjab, North Western provinces and South India had indicated that the concept of a multi-ethnic society and its central polarity had gradually acquired a definite shape in the minds of the imperial policy planners. Risley's justifications give a fairly good idea of the motives and objectives underlying the official studies into the internal organisation of Indian society:

> The native society is made up of a network of subdivisions governed by rules which affect every department of life. How that society will behave under novel conditions, what use will it make of any particular form of political representation are questions which cannot be answered without fairily minute knowledge of the internal organisation of society.[47]

In other words, a thorough knowledge of the ethnic composition of the subject society was regarded as an important aid in determining the proper representation of different segments of populations in the representative bodies. In this manner, no particular group could monopolise power. This consideration was to become increasingly important in the colonial reform policies and electoral politics in the early twentieth century India.

Ethnicity had an economic dimension as well because caste status, as Risley speculated, was often an index of wealth. Hence, an ethnographic survey would not only ensure an equitable distribution of wealth but would also facilitate the assessment of any direct tax.[48]

The British rulers were, perhaps, not enamoured of Risley's scientific interests but they sponsored his scheme of ethnographic survey with two expectations. First of all, they were searching for a depressed under-class to serve as a counter-weight to the majority Hindu community. Secondly, the colonial state was keen to acquire a more minute knowledge about the Indian society in order to face the sensitive question of social reforms without hurting the sentiments of the masses at large.[49] In order to deal effectively with the current social problems such as infanticide and to devise broad policy measures to influence the course of the social reform movements, the British rulers had decided to coordinate their 'technology of governing' in Focault's phrase[50] with the detailed knowledge about the religious and social customs of the people inhabiting village, *tehsil*, district and provincial spaces. Herbert Risley believed that the Bengal model would be applicable to the rest of India.

In fact, the British had attached a great value to the role of knowledge in the exercise of imperial power. Thus, the settlement surveys, population censuses and reports of economic and cultural practices, compiled through the British period, should not be regarded merely as products of the administrative system but a corollary to the imperial perception of the vital relationship between governability of India and knowledge about its social morphology. While advertising its object, *The Ethnographic Survey of India* (to be conducted as a part of the Indian Census, 1901) in the first volume of *Man* in 1901, stated:

> The entire framework of native life in India is made of groups of this kind (castes and tribes) and the status and conduct of individuals are largely determined by the rules of the groups to which they belong .... An ethnographic survey is as necessary an incident of good administration as a cadastral survey of the land and a record of the rights of its tenants.[51]

In accordance with this classic formulation in contemporary morphological sociology, the entire land mass of India was mapped, recorded and allotted to the newly-created landlords and old occupants and they were subjected to legal controls; similarly, the social world of India was split and reconstructed into defined caste identities and religious communities which were to be controlled by their respective rules and customs. In 1881, C.L. Tupper, who had codified the Punjab Customary Law, has also argued on the similar assumption, i.e. the Indian society, especially Punjabi society was 'primitive'. He proposed that the British Government

> ... must ascertain the level in civilisation at which your tribes, your villages or your joint families stand; and the more nearly your proposed rules of law are on a line with that level, the stronger is the presumption that they will suit real needs.[52]

Thus, Tupper had reinforced and refined the theory about the relationship between imperial knowledge of the nature of Asian societies and efficiency of its administration. A new concept of 'rule by reports/records' had been crystallised in the British colonial discourse.

It is essential to identify the points of time when it became an official policy to promote the acquisition and publication of such knowledge. It varied with various provinces. As far as the North-Western Provinces and Punjab are concerned, the cut off date is 1844, when a Memorandum of Thomason, the recently appointed Lieutenant-Governor, was circulated to all commissioners and collectors.[53]

Caste became a special target and site of knowledge for the ethnographer in the last three censuses of British India, i.e. 1911, 1921, and 1931. Their content pages reveal that caste, which had been firmly located as the essence of Hindu religion, formed a special chapter and was related with a variety of data: sex-ratio by caste, vernacular and English literacy by caste, age distribution by caste and occupational patterns. It may be said that collection and the reproduction of sociological and anthropological data about caste in the successive all-India or provincial census reports was done with a view to highlight the attributes of Indian people. This idea was first expressed in census literature in the third All India Census Survey, 1891.

What was the value of this qualified and quantified information about caste as the administrative strategy? R. Saumerz Smith has argued that the development of administrative records and survey reports in colonial India was linked to the formulation of a new strategy of political control in the second half of the nineteenth century. In his view, there was a correspondence between the gradual construction of an official understanding of Indian society and the gradual extension of the rule of law.[54] After the 1840s, caste in the village records of settlement reports became a reference point for definite customs, rights and duties particularly revenue obligation instead of each village negotiating the terms for running its own affairs.[55] Thus, village society became fragmented in 'countless statuses in knowledge and laws'.[56]

Unlike 'village community', which had the resilience to survive the ruin of empires, caste was a different kind of concept, serving different purposes. More a unit of knowledge than administration,[57] its importance for colonial administrator-turned-ethnographer lay in the fact that it embraced the whole of India and all sections of Indian society. Having limited utility as a unit for revenue assessment, it could be more easily manipulated for controlling majorities and minorities through a number of laws and constitutional measures by statutory imperial government. That was why from the 1840s onwards, the institution of caste was gradually impailed in the settlement reports and other records. But before caste or agricultural and other tribes could be used as a foci for the enactment of law, the statistical picture incorporating the colonial view of caste was to be officially constructed, published and shared by members of the ruling classes. Hence, the Indian census of the 1860s to 1930s was perfected as an instrument for breaking Indian society into a group of individuals, and then piecing it together through quasi-mathematical methods. Having composed this statistical picture of society, the British Government was no longer obliged to function through the mediation of 'powerful families' or the 'little republics' of village communities.

As the British perceived caste as a site of multipurpose information and statistical tool for generating a synthetic understanding of Indian society, all data about 'caste' was not useful for them. A careful perusal of the various census reports would show that the 'numerical' status of a caste was an important consideration for special attention. For example, the first caste census of North-Western Province (NWP) in 1865 contained statistics about the population concentration of the most numerous sub-castes of Brahmins, Kshatriyas, Vaishyas and Shudras.[58] The NWP Census of 1872 recorded numerically dominant castes by *pargana*. Out of 304 separate sub-divisions of the non-twice-born castes, it was said that the district-wise tabulation would be drafted only for 50 sub-castes which comprised the main body of the persons classed under 'other castes' as differentiated from the 'Great Castes'. In the NWP Census of 1881, provincial officials were instructed to collect data only for numerically important castes. As a result, it presented a statistical picture of the 'Eleven Large Castes', 'Ten Large Agricultural Castes' and thirty-seven castes of the non-twice-born castes whose numbers exceeded 1,000,000.[59] However, in the case of Punjab, where caste had more fluidity than elsewhere in India, owing to the presence of three interacting religious communities: Hindu, Sikh and Muslim, the multiple criteria of caste, religion and occupation was used to determine the status of individuals; the political importance of each of the three communities in the past, too, was kept in view while composing a picture of the Punjabi society. Hence, the concept of 'majority' and 'minority' was defined in terms of religion.[60] The British were also interested in recording those minorities like Aggarwals and Marwaris as they had a wide inter-regional network. Another category of minorities that figured in the population census reports had a reputation for flouting British law and order. They were grouped under the broad category of 'criminal tribes', *thugs,* etc. Such minorities, castes or tribes, as were crucial to the maintenance of law and order, were also listed in the NWP and Oudh Census of 1919 under the, instructions of the Census Commissioner.[61]

With an eye on utility for *raj* rather than progress of Indian society, the British ethnographers-cum-administrators located the large amount of information on caste divisions, caste rituals, etc., which was given in the Army recruitment handbooks on each of the 'martial races'. *The Handbook on Garhwalis,* for instance, was largely concerned with identifying the particular subdivisions of Rajputs and Brahmins which were amenable to military discipline.[62] Captain A.H. Bingley's study on *Sikhs* and Captain R.W. Falcon's *Handbook on Sikhs for the Use of Regimental Officers*, published in the 1890s, were written with the object of maximum utilisation of their fighting potential for the defence of the *raj* and territorial wars. The army officers' insistence that Sikh recruits must retain their traditional symbols or obtain them through baptismal ceremony upon joining the army revealed their keenness to intensify religious and caste-consciousness.[63]

The British ethnographers had used a variety of criteria to classify Indian population into castes. According to the Commissioner of Census, 1891, the major aim in prescribing the classification was 'as much uniformity as the nature of statistics will allow, so that the returns of each province may be dealt with on the same basis'.[64] In the earlier census reports, i.e. 1865, 1872 and 1881, *varna,* which covered the Hindus[65] throughout India, was used as a principle of classification. In 1891 census, the *varna* principle of classification was replaced by the occupational principle of classification. Denzil Ibbetson's ethnological report for Punjab was used as a model.[66] Nesfield had also formulated a theory of origin of caste to justify his application of occupation criterion.[67] According to Bernard Cohn, Nesfield's theory reflected the influence of Victorian anthropology which had emphasised material evolutionism. It fitted well into the intellectual premises of the colonial discourse justifying the British imperialism.

Herbert Risley, the Director of the Indian Census operations, 1901 dubbed the classification of castes in the 1891 Census as a 'patch work classification, in which occupation predominates, varied here and there by considerations of caste-history, tradition, ethnical affinity and geographical position'.[68] Its major defect according to Risley was the violation of rules of identity —ritual status, religious community and race. As a result, he proposed a Brahmin-centred classification, i.e. the Brahmin being the fixed point in traditional ritual hierarchy and Kshatriya, Vaishya and other castes stood in relation to him. Risley's scheme of classification[69] was given up in the next census for administrative reasons as it had encouraged fierce caste-competition in the first instance. Secondly, it did not provide a suitable grid of classificatory table which would help the colonial administrators in constructing an all-purpose conception of caste-ranking.[70]

Risley had also used the biological criteria to fix the social ranking of a caste. He not only believed in the existence of physical or racial differences but also emphasised their role in determining the social rank and distance between various castes:

> If we take a series of castes in Bengal, Bihar, the United Provinces of Agra and Oudh, or Madras, and arrange them in order of the average nasal index so that the caste with the finest nose shall be at the top and that with the coarsest at the bottom of the list, it will be found that this order substantially corresponds with the accepted order of social precedence.[71]

Risley had developed an elaborate theory to explain the social ranking of caste. In his view the caste system was the outcome of the encounter between two distinct racial groups. While one represented a light-skinned, narrow nosed 'Aryan' type the other represented the dark-skinned, broad-nosed 'Dravidian' type. The Aryans, according to this theory were not only the dominant group but also adopted the practice of hypergamy. This led to the formation of a series of intermediate groups whose social rank varied directly with the extent of purity of Aryan blood. Risley's arguments and conclusions, which had used anthropometric data as scientific proof, were challenged by later scholars P.C. Mahalanbois and G.S. Ghurye who dubbed his data and methods as faulty.[72] However, D.N. Majumdar, an anthropologist and C.R. Rao, a statistician, produced the most comprehensive investigative study with the help of anthropometric data about Bengal comprising both West Bengal and East Pakistan. Majumdar pointed out that his data and conclusion about the clustering of groups according to their social proximity in this region had confirmed his observations for Gujarat and Uttar Pradesh. He concluded that '... some correlation exists between the order of social precedence in a state or region, and the ethnic constellations based on anthropometric data.'[73] It must be pointed out that the afore-mentioned joint study highlighted the far more complex nature of relationship than the one which Risley believed that he had scientifically established. However, it must be conceded that Risley and other likeminded ethnographers felt encouraged by the popular misconceptions about the linkage between physical types and social status. For example, upper castes are universally believed to be light skinned and narrow-nosed and lower to be dark-skinned and broad nosed.

Some recent studies specifically by Iravati Karve made a detailed comparison between eight Brahmin 'subcastes' in Maharashtra on the basis of anthropometric, somatoscopic and serological data.[74] Her findings show that there is no necessary relationship between social distance and physical distance and even less surety about the linkage between caste and race. It may be said that the shift from morphological to genetical indicators gives additional support to the view that the relationship between social and physical distance is uncertain and tenuous.[75]

In the British ethnographic thinking the Indian people were readily divided into races or even into clearly recognisable physical types which were further related with social types, i.e. caste. The colonial ethnographer had manipulated scientific theories and statistical data to reduce Indian society into neat and coherent categories in order to manage the masses. A few of them disapproved of the official attempts to homegenise and regimentalise the social world to obtain precise knowledge for control. For example, L. Middleton, the Census Superintendent in Punjab, 1921, represented reaction against the prevalent ethnographic thinking :

> I had intended pointing out that there is a very wide revolt against the classification of occupational castes; that these castes have been largely manufactured and almost entirely preserved as separate castes by the British Government... We pigeonholed everyone by caste, and if we could not find a true caste for them, labelled them with the name of a hereditary occupation ... (the) Government's passion for labels and pigeon-holes has led to the crystallisation of the caste system, which except among the aristocratic castes was really very fluid under indigenous rules.[76]

It may also be pointed out that physical differences are not polarised in India but are spread over a continuum. The population cannot be readily divided into races or even into physical types. The caste system, in its turn, is a system of great complexity and anthropometric data is not an adequate tool to compose a real picture of Indian society.

IV

Conclusion

At the end of this discussion about the role of the colonial ethnography in the construction of racial, caste and religious identities, three important points emerge. Firstly, identities in

Indian society, which had remained amorphrous, indeterminate, and capable of apprehension at several levels—sub-caste, sect, dialect and region-were conceptualised as religious communities and caste-groups and categorised and quantified for political purposes by the British imperialists. The colonial ethnographer, who was called upon to assume new responsibilities in view of the increasing resistance to the British empire from the growing educated middle classes and a few socio-religious organisations, mapped out and fixed the boundaries separating religious communities, caste groups and ethnic elements, along with an exhaustive account of their biological characteristics, social customs and belief systems. The end-product was a coherent, intelligible, though distorted picture of the colonial society, whose members had to be controlled, enslaved, and conditioned to perceive themselves as communal and religious entities, their languages, science, literature and cultural traditions as gifts from the manly, intellectually superior, materially advanced and culturally dynamic Europe.

Secondly, the settlement surveys, population censuses, ethnologies, ethnographies and reports on economic and cultural practices (compiled during the colonial period) should not be regarded merely as products of the administrative system but as a corollary to the imperial perception of the relationship between the governability of India and knowledge about its social morphology. In order to enable the administrators and policy-makers to gear the imperial system of rule for exploiting the human and natural resources of the subject country, a well-calculated administrative strategy was developed over a long period wherein concept of religion as community and certain castes were deemed crucial and thus worthy of study and analysis from the angle of imperial interests. The colonial state created concepts of religious community, backward and depressed classes, reservations and communal electorates. While compiling the census reports, the colonial ethnographer converted them into categories which were defined, elaborated and given statistical substance over decades. These emerged finally as fixed social and cultural divisions incorporated in the constitutional structure of British India as illustrated by the Government of India Act, 1935.

Similarly, the numerical majorities in terms of castes became the subjects of special official reports because they could be used for managing masses. The minorities such as Aggarwals and Marwaris, having intra-regional network, martial, agricultural and commercial 'races' for their strategic and economic function and 'criminal tribes' as threats to law and order also received patronage, reward or punishment in accordance with their utility in the perception of the *raj*.

Within the framework of this strategy, the precise knowledge about horizontal and vertical divisions in Indian society along religion and caste lines as well as the system of checks and balances regulating the daily conduct of a culturally alien people, their social relationships and life-cycle ceremonies was requisite. The imperial power depended upon its bureaucratic efficiency to operate these controls without conceding substantial political and economic rights to the subject society. This strategic linkage between knowledge and the long-term imperial goal of *'hegemony'* required the breaking of castes into sub-castes, religious communities into sects, enumeration of the relevant categories with due allowance for religious competition and consequent conversions and their effect on marriages, and social customs. The entire data had to be collected, analysed and marked into separate administrative spaces: provinces, districts and parganas. As a part of this exercise, the ethnographer while constructing well-defined religious and caste identities, standardised names/caste-categories, reduced their number and evolved fixed social-hierarchies, and carved a neat pattern out of the bewildering complex of multi-religious and multi-ethnic society. As the listing and freezing of caste-identities and religious communities was done without any reference to actual reality, the 'invented' colonial society, though more intelligible to the imperial administrator-cum-ethnographer, had been deprived of its flexible cognitive system that could encompass geographical mobility. Thus, the construction of colonial ethnography had done violence to the traditional social system.

Thirdly, it may be conceded that the intervention of the colonial administrator-turned-ethnographer was certainly decisive in the identity-formation of Indians. However, the gradual development of the nationalist discourse and the parallel growth of the liberation struggle indicated that the Indian identity and communitarian consciousness departed from the colonial ethnographer's model for the subject society. Drawn into the process of the transformation of their traditions, modes of cognition, political and social formulations as well as identities, Indians forged a composite national identity, reconstructed their own past, refused to be preserved as specimens in the colonial ethnographer's museum of an archaic stage in world history. By learning to use imported social and material technologies, Raja Ram Mohan Roy, Lokmanya Tilak, M.K. Gandhi, B.R. Ambedkar and Pandit Nehru tried to restructure the image of Indian history and tradition, harnessed cultural resources for mobilising the people to overthrow the well-entrenched British rule, and redraw the contours of communitarian consciousness befitting the secular ideal in free India. The process of adjustment and accommodation among religious communities after partition and independence can very well be the theme of a separate paper.

I would like to add that ethnography as a tool for neo-imperialists has not lost its relevance even today. This is evident from the current trends in Western historiography on Asia and Africa. For example, some American scholars, the Cambridge school of historians, and a number of European scientists have not given up their favourite project of glorifying their political and scientific fitness, intellectual superiority and achievements coupled with the debunking of Asian social systems, their culture, mentalities and epistemologies. Even more dangerous is the vulnerability of the people of developed and underdeveloped countries of the third world to this propoganda. So strong is the hold of ideological enslavement that these people are easily persuaded to buy self-image, world-views, outdated products and technologies from Europe as well sign trade agreements, despite their being suicidal to their national interests. The present discussion on the relationship between the knowledge of other societies and their manipulation for imperialist profit underlines the urgency of the decolonisation of consciousness through the ongoing intellectual dialogue and its wider dissemination among the educated classes at least.

It may also be pointed out that knowledge of social morphology is increasingly being misused by Asian politicians to keep their countrymen embroiled in communal and caste-conflicts for the sake of power. I may end this discussion by raising a question. How do we emancipate ourselves from the colonial categories and slots and forge more harmonious identities?

REFERENCES

1. Kenneth W. Jones, *Arya Dharma: Hindu Consciousness in the 19th Century Punjab*, Delhi, 1977, 12.
2. Benedict Anderson, *Imagined Communities: Reflections on the Origin and Spread of Nationalism*, London, 1983, Title page.
3. Sudipta Kaviraj, *On the Construction of Colonial Power: Structure, Discourse, Hegemony*: Occasional Papers on History and Society, Second Series, no. XXXV, New Delhi: Centre for Contemporary Studies, Nehru Memorial Museum and Library, 1991, 19.
4. S. Gopal, *British Policy in India 1858-1905*, London, 1965, 7,40,302.
5. Cited in S.R. Mehrotra, *The Emergence of the Indian National Congress*, New Delhi, 1971, 305-6. Summarising the clash of two approaches, i.e. 'authoritarian' and 'liberal' principles, the Viceroy, Lord Ripon, had underlined its impact on the construction of the colonial state.
6. Sudipta Kaviraj, op. cit. (3) , 33.
7. For a discussion on 'Enlightenment' and 'European Rationalist Theory and Their Implications for Imperialism and Colonialism see Ira O. Wade, *The Structure of French Enlightenment* (Princeton, 1977), XV-XIX, 3-25.
8. Sudipta Kaviraj, op. cit. (3), 39. For an interesting discussion on this point see K.N. Panikar, *Presidential Address: Modern India*, Aligarh 1975.
9. Percival Spear, 'The British and the Indian State' in *Tradition and Politics in South Asia* (ed. R.J. Moore), New Delhi, 1979, 168-9.
10. Ibid., 161-164.

11. K.S. Vakil and S. Natrajan, *Education in India*, New Delhi, 1966, 93.
12. For Macaulay's 'Minute, 1835' see *A Source Book of Modern Indian Education* (ed. M.R. Paranjape), London, 1938, 50ff. Earlier Charles Grant had also drawn attention to the twin objectives of spreading English education: dissemination of colonial ideology and its utility for administrative needs. For his 'Observations, 1797' see ibid.
13. K.N. Panikkar, 'The Intellectual History of Colonial India: Some Historiographical and Conceptual Questions in *Situating Indian History* (eds. S. Bhattacharya and Romila Thapar), Delhi, 1986, 421. Also Sudhir Chandra : 'Literature and Colonial Consciousness', paper presented at the Seminar on *Social Transformation and Creative Imagination* (New Delhi: Nehru Memorial Museum Library, 1983). Sudhir Chandra argued that 'ambivalence' was not the product of pragmatic considerations but an integral part of the colonial consciousness.
14. Ibid., 422. Also Ram Mohan Roy, 'Final Appeal to the Christian Public' in *The English Works of Raja Ram Mohan Roy* (ed. J.C. Ghosh), Allahabad, 1905, 284-5.
15. Sudipta Kaviraj, op. cit. (3), 53.
16. Ibid. Also Rashmi Pant, 'The Cognitive Status of Caste in Colonial Ethnography: A Review of Some Literature on the North West Provinces and Oudh' *Indian Economic and Social History Review* (1987), 24, 2, 146, 148.
17. Charles E. Trevelyan, 'Education of the People of India 1838' in M.R. Paranjape, op. cit. (12), 47, 57, 62.
18. For the text of Macaulay's 'Minute, 1853' see Ibid.
19. Claude Alvares, 'Science, Colonialism and Violence: A Luddite View' in *Science, Hegemony and Violence: A Requiem for Modernity* (ed. Ashish Nandy) Delhi, 1988, 91.
20. I have borrowed this concept from Claude Alvares.
21. Cited in T. Ronald Takaki, *Iron Cages: Race and Culture in Nineteenth Century America*, New York, 1979, 261-62
22. Ibid., p. 269
23. For an overview of British and rural-tribal perspectives on the forest settlements see Neeladri Bhattacharya, 'Colonial State and Agrarian Society' in S. Bhattacharya and Romila Thapar, op. cit. (13), 117-32.
24. Robert Miles, *Racism*, London, 1989, 31.
25. Ibid., 33-35. Information reproduced in the foregoing paragraphs in based on Miles.

26. Allan Chase, *The Legacy of Malthus: The Social Costs of the New Scientific Racism*, Chicago, 1980, 72.
27. Ibid., 73-74.
28. Michael J. Cullen, *The Statistical Movement in Early Victorian Britain: The Foundations of Empirical Research*, New York, 1975, 80-81.
29. For an illuminating discussion of growth of the British self-image as a master-race and imperialism see Michael Howard, 'Empire, Race and War in pre-1914 Britain in *History and Imagination* (eds. Hugh Lloyd Jones, Valerie Pearl and Blair Warden), Duckworth, 1981, 341-9.
30. Cited in Adam Kuper, *The Invention of Primitive Society*, London, 1988, 2.
31. Ibid.
32. George W. Stocking, *Victorian Anthropology* London, 1987, 124-125.
33. Ranajit Guha, *A Rule of Property: An Essay on the Permanent Settlement*, Paris, 1963, p. 26.
34. P. Padamnabha, *Anthropology and Anthropologist*, London, 1983, 103.
35. P. Padamnabha, *Indian Census and Anthropological Investigations*, New Delhi, 1978, p. 175.
36. *Herbert Risley Papers* (microfilm; New Delhi, National Archives of India), Reel 1, letter of Sir Michael Forster to the British Association of Advancement of Science, December, 1899.
37. H.H. Risley, On the Application of Dr. Topinard's Anthropometric System to the Tribes and Castes of Bengal, Rungpore, dated March 8, 1887, 83-85. Cited in Sekhar Bandhopadhyay, 'The Raj, Risley and Tribes and Castes of Bengal' *India Past and Present*, 1985, 2,1,44.
38. Ibid., 86 - Letter from W.H. Flower, F.R.S., Director, British Museum, Natural History Department to H.H. Risley, on Special Duty, dated August 8, 1886, financial (Misc) March 188-96.
39. H.H. Risley 'Ethnographic Enquiries Bengal', dated Darjeeling, December 22, 1886, Financial (Misc.), March 1887, p. 27. Cited in Sekhar Bandopadhyay, op. cit. (37).
40. H.H. Risley, op. cit. (36), 85.
41. Ibid.
42. E.A. Gait, Census of India, 1911 I (Calcutta, 1913), 381. Also R.E. Enthoven, *The Tribes and Castes of Bombay*, First published 1920: Reprinted Delhi: Cosmo Publications, 1975, Introduction,

pp. viii & ix, and Appendix, for an insightful study of the British discourse of differentiation see B.S. Cohn 'Notes on the Study of Indian Society and Culture' in *Structure and Change in Indian Society* (eds. Milton Singer and B.S. Cohn), Chicago 1968, 6-15.

43. H.H. Risley distinguished seven physical types (excluding the small group of negritos in the Andamans) namely, (i) The Turko-Iranian type on the North-West (ii) The Indo-Aryan type of the Punjab, Rajputana and Kashmir (iii) The Scytho-Dravidian type of western India (iv) The Aryo-Davidian type of the United Provinces and Bihar (v) The Mongolo Dravidian type of Bengal and Orissa (vi) The Dravidian type of Madras, Hyderabad, the Central Provinces, Central India and Chota Nagpur. Our present condition of knowledge regarding the relative permanence of various physical characteristics does not permit us to draw any conclusion regarding the ancestry of the Indian people and the superiority of the European people on the basis of cephalic and nasal indices and skin colour. The history of migrations of castes and tribes in India and influence of the environments on the physique of the people living in different parts of globe has not yet been fully studied. Hence, any definitive view on races, castes and tribes needs to be based on a more suphisticated and reliable data.
44. The Criminal Tribes Legislation, which developed from early twentieth century, necessitated compulsory finger-printing and restrictions on mobility.
45. Sekhar Bandopadhyay, 'Caste in the Perception of the Raj: A Note on the Evolution of Colonial Sociology in Bengal' *Bengal Past and Present* (1985), civ, pts. I & II, 198-199, 60.
46. Ibid., 76 - Letter from H.L. Dampier, Additional Secretary to the Government of Bengal, to the Secretary to the Government of India, Home Department. File no. 455, February 2, 1869 (General).
47. H.H. Risley, *The Tribes and Castes of Bengal*, 4 vols., 1891-1896, i, Calcutta, 1891, vii.
48. H.H. Risley, 'Ethnographic Enquiries', 31.
49. Resolution of Government of Bengal, Financial Department, 30 April, 1885, Financial, (Miscellaneous) Proceedings, March, 1887, p. 36. cited in Sekhar Bandopadhyay, op. cit. (45), 67-68.
50. Michel Foucault, *Ideology and Consciousness*, London, 1979, 5-21. In his discussion of governmentality, Foucault has discussed the evolution of the 'technologies of governing' in Europe in which household, from being a model of state, became a privileged

instrument of state control. This served as a unit for the collection of statistics and a point for relating the individual with the state. In the context of the British rule, the introduction of official use of statistics in land-revenue administration, later in population census and other reports and records, made the Indian society intelligible and organised into a neat pattern.

51. *Census of India, 1901, Report,* 138.
52. C.L. Tupper, *Punjab Customary Law* 1881, 46.
53. Richard Saumarez Smith 'Rule-by-records and rule-by-reports: complementary aspects of the British Imperial rule of law' *Contributions to Indian Sociology*, 19,1,156.
54. Ibid., 163.
55. Ibid., 169-171.
56. Ibid., 163.
57. Ibid., 173.
58. The first North Western Provinces Census (1853) counted and recorded the number of Hindus and Muslims separately. But the caste and occupation were not added until the next census in 1872. A similar practice, followed in the Punjab Census, indicates that religion was the primary concern for the colonial administrators-cum-ethnographers and it was given more space and weightage in the compilation of reports and statistical tables. The second and third Punjab censuses in 1868, 1891 respectively are good examples.
59. *Census of India*, 1881, Report, 277, 281-2.
60. Kamlesh Mohan 'Constructing Religion and Caste and Manipulating Identities (19th to early 20th century)' *Social Sciences Research Journal* (March-July, 1992), 1-2, 152.
61. *Census of India 1881, Report,* 278. Also Rashmi Pant, op. cit. (16) 150.
62. Captain J. Evatt, *Garhwalis* (1894). This handbook for the Indian Army was revised by Ltd. Col. K. Henderson, 1941.
63. Joyce Pettigrew, *Robber Noblemen: A Study of the Political System of the Sikh Jats*, London, 1975, 41-43. She has suggested that the British army policy had played an intensifying and sustaining role in Sikh identity-formation. However, W.H. McLeod has emphasised the primary significance of the army policy in the 'economic opportunity that it afforded' in his book *The Evolution of the Sikh Community*, Oxford, 1976, 55.
64. *Census of India, 1891, Report*, 188. The Chief Census Commissioner also suggested here that the same caste was divided by religion, as for example, Jats into Hindus, Muslims and Sikhs, Baniyas

into Hindus and Jain, or tribals professing a variety of religions from Animism to Christianity; *'the latter fact should be recognised as well as the social distinction'* (italics mine).

65. For a comparative view see *Census of India*, 1865, 1872 and 1891, *Report*, especially the chapter on 'Religion'. Apart from Hindus, there were separate categories in the census for Sikhs, Jains, Aryas, Muslims and Christians. *The Punjab Census Report*, 1891 had also identified the major sects or orders in each religion and its sub divisions. For example, Hinduism was subdivided into Orders of *yogis* and *sanyasis*. Islam was sub-divided into Sunnis, Shias and Wahabis by percentage and Christians were split into Anglicans, Baptists, Presbyterians, Roman Catholics and unspecified.
66. For the table of classification by occupation see Denzil Ibbetson, *Punjab Castes*, reprinted, Delhi, 1981.
67. J.C. Nesfield, *A Brief View of the Caste System of NWP and Oudh*, Allahabad, 1885, 114-5.
68. *Census of India*, 1901, *Report*, 538.
69. For Risley's scheme see *Census of NWP and Oudh*, 1901; 2 vols., i. 216. For his justification of Brahmin-centred scheme see p. 556.
70. Rashmi Pant, op. cit, (16), 159.
71. H.H. Risley, *The People of India*, Calcutta, 1908, 29.
72. P.C. Mahalanobis, 'A Revision of Risley's anthropometric data, *Samkhya*, I (1933), 76-105. Also G.S. Ghurye, *Caste and Race in India*, London, 1932, 102-3.
73. D.N. Majumdar and C.R. Rao, *Race Elements in Bengal: A Quantitative Study*, Calcutta, 1960, 102-3.
74. Irawati Karve, *Hindu Society, An Interpretation* (Poona, 1961), 114-5.
75. Andre Beteille, 'Race, Caste and Ethnic Identity' in *Race, Science and Society* (ed. Leo Kuper) London, 1975, 221.
76. L. Middleton, *Census of India, Punjab 1921*. Cited in S.C. Ghurye, *Caste and Class in India* (Bombay, 1957), 195.

2

The Development of Modern Sciences in the Panjab University under Colonial Rule, 1882-1947

The annexation of the kingdom of Lahore in the final phase of the British conquest of India in 1849 removed the last pocket of resistance to the establishment of Pax Britannica. Henceforth, the British rulers sought to colonise the economy, and the cultural and intellectual heritage of India. More significant than the introduction of new methods of land surveys, revenue assessment and collection was the grafting of Western institutional structures for administration, education and forms of knowledge.

In this chapter, I shall argue that science and technology became powerful instruments in the effective exercise and legitimisation of the colonial state and its power, as well as in the development of the imperial map of India. This objective was achieved through a systematic diffusion of Western sciences and technology. Borrowing Shiv Vishvanathan's hypothesis regarding the development of science and technology in colonial India, it may be divided into three phases.[1] The first phase, launched in the mid-eighteenth century, was described as the era of 'great surveys'. Conducted on a scientific basis, a wide range of topographical, statistical, trigonometric, cartographic and other surveys had a long-term significance not only for the scientific mapping of India, but also for the development of scientific knowledge in Britain and Europe.

The second phase led to the introduction of scientific and technical education in colonial India. Known for the famous Anglicist-Orientalist controversy in 1835, it had crucial significance for the formulation of goals and direction of the policy for the development of science and technology in India. The third and the final phase was marked by the colonial state's calculated attempts to forge institutional links between science, technology and the Indian economy. Primarily consisting of experiments in building scientific institutions, it had a potential role in the development of Indian society and rational thinking and attitudes among the people.

This chapter deals with the diffusion of Western sciences and technology in the second phase, which was notable for the establishment of universities in the Presidency towns of Calcutta, Bombay and Madras in 1857 and 25 years later in Lahore, the capital of Panjab (now Punjab). The primary focus of analysis shall be the development of Western (often regarded as synonymous with modern) sciences in the Panjab University from 1882 to 1947. In this context, it is relevant to outline briefly the growth and expansion of the university with special reference to the establishment of science departments and the development of their infrastructure. Individual contributions towards the development of major subjects, namely botany, mathematics, chemistry and physics, and stimulating interest in science research shall be discussed.

I

Beginnings and Expansion of Panjab University

The demand for a university in the Panjab had its genesis in a letter dated June 10, 1865 from Sir Donald McLeod, the then lieutenant-governor of the Province, inviting suggestions for 'the improvement of Oriental learning and the development of a sound vernacular literature'.[2] The *Anjuman-i-Panjab,* which had originally proposed the setting up of an 'Oriental University', extended support to the establishment of 'an Anglo Oriental institution' in the Punjab.

> [Its] first object should be to develop the literature of the classical and modern languages of northern India and the next object should be to convey a knowledge of essential European learning and science through the languages of the people so far as that should be possible while preserving a standard of attainment which should ensure its recognition as a true university.[3]

To cut a long story short, the British Government, opposed to the idea of establishing a university immediately, raised the Government College of Lahore (established in 1864) to the status of a University College.[4] The Panjab University College came into existence by Notification No. 472, dated December 8, 1869, along with statutes of the institution. One of the special objects of this college was 'to promote the diffusion of European sciences'.[5] Almost one decade and a half elapsed before Act No. XIX of Incorporation was passed by the Legislative Council in 1882, leading to the establishment of Panjab University in Lahore. Baden Powell was appointed the first Vice-Chancellor and Dr. G.W. Leitner the Registrar of the new university. Dr. Leitner had been working as the Principal of the Oriental College and Registrar of the Panjab University College since 1870, and continued in that capacity for the university till November 1885.

The Panjab University differed radically from the older universities of India, namely Calcutta, Bombay and Madras. First, it did not owe its origin entirely to the state government's efforts but was a product of the initiative and intensive drive of Dr. G.W. Leitner, eminent citizens, the Princes and Europeans. Second, the governing body of the university, or the Senate, was more representative in character than the Senates of the older universities. It functioned as 'an advisory body to the Panjab Government, a position hitherto not occupied by any of the other existing universities of India'. Third, it was a teaching as well as an examining body. It maintained its own institutions, namely the Oriental College and the Law School, and had been authorized to establish 'such other schools and colleges as the Senate may from time to time direct'. Fourth, the university became a unique synthesis of the Oriental and Western systems of education. It had the mandate to provide special encouragement to Oriental studies along with imparting education in the higher branches of Western sciences and knowledge-system through the medium of modern Indian languages. The university had also adopted the Western system of education, and the English language was used as a medium of instruction.[6]

The story of the growth of the Panjab University from 1882 to 1904 is nothing but a record of the conduct of examinations and the affiliation of educational institutions. In its base outline, the university performed four functions—as an examining body, as an advisory body of education for the Provincial Government, as a managing body for a College for Oriental Studies and a Law School, and as an affiliating body for the fast-growing number of educational institutions. Its records show that the university, in its early phase of development, was primarily an examining and administrative body. In 1902, only 27 per cent of its expenditure was upon teaching and less than 5 per cent upon its libraries. Almost nothing was spent on the encouragement of literature. In spite of the fact that the university had been empowered to confer degrees in science subjects as early as 1906, little provision had been made for teaching science subjects in any college except the Medical College and the Government College, Lahore. Ever since its establishment in 1860, the Medical College had provided its own preliminary instruction to the medical students in general science, basic to medicine. In 1905, the university proposed to transfer elementary instruction in science from the Medical College to the curriculum of the Science Faculties of the university. In 1906, the university instituted the degree of Master of Science (MSc), which gave great impetus to advanced study and research in Sciences at the Government College of Lahore. The dual system of examinations was also abolished because it placed a double burden on students. Henceforth, they were not required to appear at the examinations, conducted by the University of Calcutta, for the award of a degree.

At this point, it is relevant to highlight the contribution of Panjab University College (better known as Government College), Lahore, in the promotion of teaching and research in science, while Punjab University was still in the process of becoming a 'teaching corporation'. Its faculty members had either been recruited through the Indian Education Service (the majority of them being Englishmen—graduates and postgraduates from the Universities of Oxford and Cambridge) or Provincial Education Service, started after education was classified as a 'Transferred' subject under the scheme of Dyarchy in the Government of India Act 1919. In the early phase of its development, teaching was the primary function, hence Europeans/Englishmen possessing a BA or an MA degree were appointed as professors and principals. For example, W.H. Crank (earlier Principal of La Martiniere College, Lucknow) was given the chair of mathematics in 1865 and T.W. Lindsay succeeded him in 1869. In 1877, J. Sime, appointed as Principal in 1877, taught mathematics. T.C. Lewis, MA, was appointed as Professor of mathematics. In 1881, Golak Nath Chatterji (BA) was recruited as assistant professor and Rai Bahadur S.B. Mukerji as professor. On his retirement in 1898, Mukerji was succeeded by G.N. Chatterji.[8] Obviously, research was not on the agenda up to the turn of the century. The department of mathematics became vibrant in the area of research with the appointment of Bhai Gopal Singh Chawla as assistant professor in 1902. After taking his Tripos in Trinity College, Cambridge, he was promoted as senior professor of mathematics in 1918. A few years later, he was elevated to the Indian Education Service. In recognition of his services, the British Government conferred upon him the title of Rai Bahadur. After his death in January 1930, his obituary, published in Volume 18 of the *Journal of the Indian Mathematical Society* in 1930, mentioned his active association with the Indian Mathematical Society since 1909, and as its joint secretary during 1927-29. A Brahmo and a committed social reformer, Gopal Singh was also a trustee of Dyal Singh College, Lahore.[9]

Sarvadaman Chawla (his foreign colleagues spelt it as 'Chowla'), whose keen aptitude for numbers had been nurtured by his father Gopal Singh, passed his MA in 1928 from the Government College, Lahore. After finishing his Ph.D. from Trinity College, Cambridge, under Professor J.E. Littlewood,

Sarvadaman Chawla returned to India in 1931 to join as lecturer at St. Stephen's College, Delhi. In the course of his short stint at the Banaras Hindu University in 1932, he was invited by Dr. Radhakrishnan to take up a position as reader and head of the department of mathematics at Waltair in 1932. In 1936, he joined as professor at the Government College, Lahore, where his father had previously enjoyed this honour. Chawla's contribution to the advancement of knowledge towards the Number Theory in mathematics and his inspirational role in training students for research will be discussed while reviewing the achievements of the eminent scientists who were associated with the Panjab University as students, teachers and researchers.[10]

Turning to the development of the departments of physics, chemistry, botany and zoology, one is struck by the indifference and niggardliness of the Punjab Government as well as of the agenda of the British Government. Despite the insistent popular demand for opportunities and facilities for the teaching of modern sciences, no appointments were made. J.C. Oman was the first to be appointed as professor of physical science in 1877, and continued up to 1897. Ruchi Ram Sahni (1863-1948) joined as assistant professor of science in 1877, and continued up to 1897. Ruchi Sahni joined as assistant professor of science in 1885.[11] In the *History of Gazetted Officers* (Punjab Civil List Section), Ruchi Ram Sahni was shown as officiating professor of science till 1898 (confirmed in his post in 1906),[12] and Lala Khushi Ram, MA, also occupied the same position.[13]

As the colonial government was not interested in promoting the development of scientific talent among Indian students, adequate funds were not sanctioned for building well-equipped and independent laboratories for each science subject. In fact, provision was made for the teaching of general science and not physics and chemistry as separate subjects. Appointed in May 1898, Professor A.S. Hemmy held the combined chair of physics and chemistry up to 1906,[14] when B. Mouat Jones, MA, from Balliol College, Oxford, was appointed as professor of chemistry. Lala Chetan Anand, MA, of the Aitcheson Chief's College, was appointed as assistant professor of physics.[15] As there were no laboratories, no practical examinations were held.

The first chemistry laboratory was built in 1901, and enlarged in 1910-11 to treble the accommodation and bring all the arrangements up-to-date. By this time the number of science students had risen from 87 (49 in physics and 38 in chemistry) to 295 in 1911. These figures included the number of students in Physics, Chemistry and Biology. After 1906, the teaching of chemistry and physics, shared by A.S. Hemmy, Ruchi Ram Sahni and Chetan Anand, were separated. Professor Hemmy took the department of physics and Professor Jones was given the charge of chemistry. Chetan Anand was attached with A.S. Hemmy and Ruchi Ram Sahni concentrated on chemistry. MA classes (the MSc degree dated only from 1908) were already being held. The chemistry department added not only to its material assets but also to its teaching staff with the creation of a second professorship and the post of a demonstrator. Former assistant professor Ruchi Ram Sahni was promoted to the second professorship in 1909. Besides, his outstanding contribution to the Lahore Exhibition in 1909 earned him the title of 'Rai Sahib'. The retirement of Professor Jones in 1912 led to the induction of Professor B.S. Wilsdon.[16]

The teaching of science was strengthened by a change in the regulations for the medical degrees of Panjab University in 1902. For admission to the Medical College, an Intermediate in Science (ISc) instead of the simple BA was made a compulsory qualification. It was decided by the government that teaching of pure science should be made a speciality of the Government College of Lahore. As a result, intermediate classes in biology and zoology were started in the college. For this purpose, teachers had to be appointed in these two subjects. To begin with, H.M. Chhibber, MA, was inducted as assistant professor of biology. He had not only to teach biology and zoology, but also to supervise the practical work for the two subjects.[17] It may be pointed out that the colonial administrators conveniently used the term 'biology' to denote the natural history sciences of zoology and botany which deal with living things, as distinguished from those other sciences which dealt with inorganic substances. H.L.O. Garrett was critical of the official approach of lumping together various sciences under a convenient term. He observed,

> [T]his idea dominating the minds of the authorities in the heroic attempt that was being made to teach under this title (Biology), two subjects, each requiring laboratory work up to the standard of the BSc degree, in one room and by means of one single teacher. Though magnificent, *this was not education.*[18]

Till 1906, biology and zoology remained a combined subject. With the transfer of H.M. Chhibber to Bombay Presidency during the vacation of this year, Captain J. Stephenson, IMS (then Civil Surgeon of Ambala), was temporarily appointed against the existing vacancy. Shiv Ram Kashyap, BSc, was appointed as assistant professor. As a convenient arrangement, Captain Stephenson was given zoology and Shiv Ram Kashyap (who had a degree in physiology) was assigned to teach botany. Behari Lal Bhatia, BSc, again a physiologist, was also appointed as assistant professor[19].

Without going into the details of the changes in the syllabus of science and the provision of accommodation and apparatus for practical classes in botany and zoology, it is relevant to refer to the generous help provided in the form of specimens from their Zoological Collection by the Medical College. In fact, the Medical College generously transferred the whole of the Zoological Museum to the biology department. The paltry annual grants by the Punjab Government hampered the expansion of infrastructure, and thus of the teaching and research programme in science subjects. Despite these handicaps, an MSc class in zoology was started, but discontinued soon after. In the botany department, an MSc class could only be started in 1912 when Shiv Ram Kashyap (who had done his MSc degree from Panjab University in 1910) returned after earning a Tripos in natural sciences from Cambridge.[20] While he was appointed professor of botany, Bishambher Das (officiating as assistant professor during Kashyap's absence) was given a permanent appointment.

It is evident that the Government College, Lahore, as the University College and in its own capacity, played a difficult but valuable role in arousing and sustaining interest in acquiring knowledge in sciences, especially physics, chemistry, biology and zoology, in view of the inadequate funding and discriminatory recruitment policy towards Indians, however talented. Library and laboratory facilities did not match either the requirements of the increasing number of students or the keenness of talented faculty members like Shiv Ram Kashyap, Ruchi Ram Sahni, Gopal Singh Chawla and Sarvadaman Chawla to do more.

II

Development of Sciences from the 1920s to the 1940s

Growth of nationalist sentiment and anger against the scarcities during the inter-war period (1914-19), as well as against the insensitive and brutal handling of the anti-Rowlatt agitation in the Punjab, had a dampening effect on the expansion of the Government College, Lahore, which provided instruction in arts and sciences as an extended centre of Panjab University. The other constituent colleges, namely the Forman Christian College, Islamia College and D.A.V. College, had also participated in stimulating interest in higher education among the middle classes.

The beginning of a new phase in the growth of Panjab University from the 1920s onwards was due to two reasons. First, it was felt that the influence of the Panjab University was far too mechanical and was spreading widely among the middle classes without setting high standards of achievement.[21] The need to develop the cultural influence of the University was one of the themes addressed by the Chancellor, Sir Michael O'Dwyer, in 1917. The second reason was the introduction of Dyarchy under the Government of India Act of 1919, which classified education as a 'Transferred' subject while retaining European education as a 'Reserved' subject. It enabled Sir John Maynard (also the Finance Member in the Punjab Government) to establish Honours Schools in Arabic, Sanskrit, Botany and Zoology in Lahore, and in Mathematics at Delhi. Appointments of professors were also sanctioned in pursuit of the decision to convert Panjab University into a 'teaching corporation'. Hence, S.R. Kashyap, professor of botany at the Government College, was appointed professor-in-chief, and Birbal Sahni[22] as professor of botany at the university. Mr C.V.H. Rao was appointed professor of mathematics, W.H. Myles professor of economics, C.L. Boulenger professor-in-chief in the Honours School in Zoology, and Mr. Lakshman Swarup as professor of Sanskrit in the Oriental College. G. Mathai, who succeeded Colonel J. Stephenson as professor of zoology in the Government College, was nominated a University Professor in that subject.[23] More significant achievements in 1919-23 were the establishment of teaching departments of its own by the Panjab University, as well as the institution of an Academic Council and the provision for affiliated Intermediate Colleges.[24]

Having committed to transforming itself into a 'teaching corporation', the university engaged in three kinds of activity. These were: the logical addition of more teaching departments; the progressive provision of buildings and equipment for housing these departments and incorporated colleges and for the residence of students; and collaboration and coordination between the university teaching departments and the local colleges of Lahore, so as to pool their respective resources.[25] of the three aspects of the new policy, the first had been developed further since its initiation. Hence, an elaborately designed and well-equipped department of chemistry was established in 1922-23. Around the same time, a University Chemical Laboratory was constructed in consultation with H.B. Dunncliff and Bawa Kartar Singh of the local Government College. In May 1924, Dunncliff was given the title and status of University Professor of inorganic chemistry. In the following year, Shanti Swarup Bhatnagar was appointed to the department as professor of physical chemistry and Director of the Laboratories. In the same year, the university appointed a reader in organic chemistry. Thus, in a very short span of time, the Panjab University was in a position to establish a full-fledged department of chemistry, containing subsections of physical, organic and technical chemistry. It had already completed the building of an observatory and a department of astronomy in 1921, and had taken over the departments of zoology and botany of the Government College, Lahore, as also its professors in these subjects. I need not go into details regarding the provision of buildings and equipment for the accommodation of the teaching departments in arts and Oriental languages, which formed the second most important activity in the new policy for diffusing and extending knowledge.[26] The third line of activity was concerned with the 'collaboration and coordination between the University teaching departments and the local colleges of Lahore, so as to pool their resources'. It had a significant bearing upon teaching and research in various streams of science and arts. In this respect, the innovative arrangements for inter-collegiate cooperation for teaching, guiding and training students in the university teaching departments at the initial stages proved very fruitful.[27]

The relationship between Panjab University and Government College, Lahore, was based upon considerations of mutual advantage. Mian Afzal Hussain once described them as a 'pair of inseparables'.[28] The college did most of the university's work and the university was content, on the whole, with its role as an examining and a diploma-awarding body. Headships of some of the university departments were held by Government College professors, and the university departments of zoology and botany functioned in the laboratories of the Government College. Even the undergraduate classes in these two subjects, managed by the university for students of all the affiliated Lahore colleges, were mainly taught by Government College teachers. This was a good example of inter-collegiate coordination and pooling of their resources. However, the Government College maintained its lead in many ways in the sciences. The university department of physics started as an extension of the physics department of this college. The best among the students, who attended the university for instruction, were enrolled at the Government College. It was proudly proclaimed on the occasion of the Silver Jubilee celebrations in 1933 that three among the six recipients of honorary degrees, Manohar Lal, Muhammad Iqbal and Shiv Ram Kashyap, were former

Government College students. In 1935, the university began to take over the functions of advanced teaching and research in science. A beginning was made with the establishment of the departments of zoology and botany in this year.[29]

The Silver Jubilee celebrations of the university coincided with the appointment by the British Government of the Panjab University Enquiry Committee 'to enquire into and report on the reform of the University'. After making a systematic survey of the conditions of the university from October 1932 to March 1933, it recommended measures for its improvement. In February 1934 the Senate, while considering the recommendation of the Panjab University Enquiry Committee, resolved '... that the medium of instruction and examination in the 10 years' course (Matriculation) shall be Vernacular, subject to such exceptions as may have to be made in the case of European schools or individuals'.[30] For this purpose, Urdu, Hindi and Punjabi were recognised by the university, holding out scope for the inclusion of other vernaculars from time to time. However, its implementation was delayed due to official prevarication in sanctioning the proposed amendment.

No positive gain accrued to the development of science subjects in the Panjab University. Arising out of the recommendations of the Enquiry Committee, an Experts' Committee was appointed to advise the university about the continuance of an Honours School in Technical Chemistry. On its recommendation, it was abolished. Its courses were integrated with the curriculum of the Honours School in Chemistry, and an MSc degree in technology was instituted. The arrangements for university teaching in the subject were made in the Forman Christian College (one of the constituent colleges of Panjab University) on an annual subsidy of Rs 27,000.[31] Another addition to the teaching of science subjects was the institution of a Degree in Dental Surgery and a Diploma in Laryngology (the branch of medicine concerned with the larynx and its diseases) and Octology.[32]

The outbreak of World War II seriously retarded the programme of the expansion of Panjab University. India was dragged into the conflict between imperialist powers, much against her will. In the *Panjab University Annual Report for the Year 1940-41*, it was recorded that 'in view of the grave international situation, the Senate placed at the disposal of the Government all their resources for war purposes. Even the University Chemical Laboratories were placed at the disposal of the Government for defence work.'[33] The university students did not remain unaffected by the Quit India Movement either. Their anti-imperialist sentiments were articulated through protests, processions and strikes on one pretext or the other. A few minor developments of the Panjab University in academic fields, such as appointments to higher teaching posts and the introduction of a few new subjects of study, lost their significance against the backdrop of the national struggle for independence and communal riots.

In 1943 Sir John Sergeant, then Educational Adviser to the Government of India, was asked by the Reconstruction Committee of the Viceroy's Executive Council to prepare a memorandum on post-war Educational Development in India.[34] The major suggestion in this memorandum (popularly known as the Sergeant Report), concerned with the urgent need for a long-range British educational policy, could never be implemented as the British imperialist rulers left with the Independence of India in August 1947. The province of Punjab was partitioned between the two independent nations—India and Pakistan. What happened to the parent University of Punjab, Lahore, as a result of the partition and the rehabilitation of the East Panjab University is beyond the scope of this chapter.

III

Contributions of Individual Scientists

The preceding narrative of the development of modern sciences in the Panjab University before partition demonstrated clearly that a number of constraints, such as the imperialist ideology and goals as well as the lack of grants for establishing science departments and building the essential infrastructures, had slowed down the process of diffusion of scientific knowledge in India. The experience of all sections of Punjabis regarding the origin and expansion of the university was no different from those in the Presidencies of Calcutta, Madras and Bombay. Despite these handicaps, a number of talented Punjabi young men worked hard to contribute substantially to the growth of sciences, particularly in the fields of mathematics, chemistry, botany and physics globally. Realising the impossibility of advanced study and research in the colonial set-up in India, they moved out to American and British universities. The following discussion of the toil and struggle of individual scientists, whose innovative work received international recognition, underlines their problems and predicaments in the pursuit of scientific knowledge in a colonial regime.

Ruchi Ram Sahni (1863-1948), an alumnus and later a teacher in the Government College, Lahore, has recently been retrieved from obscurity for his innovative contribution to the popularisation of science in pre-Independence India. Professor J.C. Oman, who built the departments of physics and chemistry in that college, not only influenced Sahni deeply, but also helped to shape his professional career. Sahni has expressed his admiration for his mentor in his *Memoirs of an Octogenarian:* 'He knew the knack of creating in the dullest of his students a lively interest in science, which meant at that time only Physics and Chemistry, Biology (subsuming Botany and Zoology) was introduced long after he had left in 1896.'[35] Despite Sahni's deep interest in mathematics, he had been motivated to choose physics and chemistry for his MA. In those days, following the tradition of Oxford and Cambridge Universities, BA and MA instead of BSc and MSc degrees used to be offered, even for science subjects.

Professor Oman enabled Ruchi Ram to escape his predicament when, as a student of MA, he was reluctant to join his post as a Second Assistant Reporter (to the British Government) in the Meteorological Department owing to his interest in a teaching assignment and in research. Aware of the bias of the colonial authorities against the appointment of Indians to teaching jobs, he advised him to join the Meteorological Department and return to a teaching assignment whenever it was available. Oman argued that it would give

Sahni an opportunity to complete his MA from the Presidency College, Calcutta. On his mentor's advice, Sahni joined the Meteorological Department and worked under Sir H.F. Blanford (brother of Sir W.T. Blanford of the Geological Survey of India). The *Pioneer* of Allahabad carried articles criticizing his appointment, arguing that Indians were not fit for such a prestigious responsibility, which involved the preparation of 'daily' and 'monthly' reports. His critics were silenced when he carried out his duties efficiently, and also predicted an impending cyclone originating in the Bay of Bengal.[36]

For many Indians including Ruchi Ram Sahni, living in a big city like Calcutta, was in itself 'a continuous source of inspiration'.[37] It proved useful in two ways. First, his interest in chemistry grew into a passion under the inspiring guidance of Professor Alexander Pedler in the classroom and laboratory of Presidency College, where he was a student. During this period, he not only formed a lifelong association with his aforesaid mentor, but also with his class-fellow Ashutosh Mookerjee, who later became the Vice-Chancellor of Calcutta University. Upendra Kishore Roy, his class fellow, strengthened his Brahmo sympathies. Second, the idea of his future role as a crusader for scientific awareness crystallised while listening to the public lectures of Jagadish Chandra Bose, P.C. Ray and Father E. Lafont at the Indian Association for the Cultivation of Science, Calcutta. This institute inspired Ruchi Ram Sahni to set up the Punjab Science Institute in collaboration with J.C. Oman, his colleague at the Government College, Lahore, in 1885.[38] Meanwhile, his appointment in 1887 as assistant professor at the Government College, Lahore (also known as University College), facilitated his engagement with teaching as well as research, and above all the popularisation of science activities. Dissemination of scientific awareness in a colonial society implied a sound theoretical understanding of the subject, ability for its practical application and demonstration, as well as a talent for the lucid transmission of factual knowledge to people of average intelligence in their own idiom. Even more daunting was the lack of organisational and institutional structures to aid the popularisation of science among the people. Moreover, it was difficult for any Indian to receive state patronage or funding for projects concerned with the dissemination of scientific awareness and the promotion of advanced research.

Despite all these handicaps, Ruchi Ram Sahni had already taken the first step by establishing the Punjab Science Institute in mid-1885. The original aim and objective of the Institute was the popularisation of all kinds of scientific knowledge throughout the Punjab by means of lectures (in English and vernacular languages), illustrated with experiments and lantern slides, as well as the publication of tracts. These objects, according to Ruchi Ram Sahni, were expanded to include the encouragement of technical education, in particular that of technical industries.[39] Pursuing the original objective, that of the dissemination of scientific awareness, Sahni managed to involve several teachers from local colleges in the activities of the Institute, especially in its lecture programme. For example, Professor Oman, the secretary of the institute, delivered several lectures on various aspects of 'Electricity' and 'Magnetism'. Dr. C.C. Caleb, who was on the faculty of the Medical College, gave a series of lectures on anatomy. Dr. Grant's lectures on 'Soap Bubbles' and 'Spinning Tops' were particularly well-received. Sahni himself delivered as many as 500 lectures in various towns of the Punjab, and repeated these in private gatherings on personal invitation from local elites. His lectures on the weather with special reference to India were based on sound and practical knowledge, which he had acquired in the course of his job as the second assistant meteorological reporter to the Government of India. Through public lectures under the auspices of the Institute, Ruchi Ram Sahni had aroused a 'real furore of enthusiasm in the province about scientific studies', and it enabled him to carry his crusade to the Princely States of Patiala, Kapurthala, Mandi and Bahawalpur as well.[40]

Another of Sahni's contributions was underlining the positive role of regional languages in the dissemination of scientific knowledge among the masses. Despite the fact that perceptions of the educated elite in Punjab during the 1880s had been influenced by the West-oriented Brahmo leaders of the Bengal renaissance (a concept that is increasingly being questioned), as the century drew to its close, they turned increasingly to indigenous sources for inspiration and strength. Hence Punjabi was assigned a valuable role for social and intellectual regeneration. Ruchi Ram preferred the use of Punjabi as a vehicle for scientific knowledge in his popular lectures. Judging by the response of his audience, including ordinary people and the elite, Sahni concluded that the mother tongue was the best medium through which to communicate modern science. It would enable people to adapt scientific knowledge and technologies to their environment, and finally contribute to the development of alternate technologies. Local languages were best suited to the effective dissemination of scientific knowledge among the masses. This was a deep-rooted conviction, shared by Indian intellectuals like Raja Ram Mohan Roy, Master Ram Chandra, and his contemporary Sir Syed Ahmed Khan.[41] There was a definite political agenda underlying the translation of the best European writings into Indian languages when Sir Syed Ahmed Khan pleaded that : 'Those bent on improving and bettering India must remember the only way of compassing [sic] this is by having the whole of arts and sciences translated into their languages'.[42]

The strongest arguments in favour of the translation project was that the constant use of the English language by impressionable children would not only habituate them to express their thoughts in it, but also 'denationalise' them. Both Ruchi Ram Sahni and Master Ram Chandra had expressed anxious concern for the growing alienation of the younger generation, whose patriotic feelings ought to be nurtured. Both of them had actively contributed to the building of 'national character'. While the former devoted his energy and talent to the translation of a number of European works on science in Urdu, the latter popularised information about the latest inventions and various branches of scientific knowledge through his lectures in Punjabi, the most widely spoken language in this region.[43]

One of the pioneers of scientific studies in Botany, Shiv Ram Kashyap (1882-1934) was a product of the Panjab University and joined the Government College, Lahore, in 1909. As we saw above, he was appointed professor of botany through the Provincial Education Service in the same college after getting his Tripos in natural sciences from Cambridge University in 1912, and was promoted to the Indian Education Service in 1920. In 1922, when the Honours School in Botany was established in the Panjab University, he was given this position, which he continued to occupy till his death in November 1934. He became the Dean of Faculty of Sciences and later the Dean of University from 1931-34. Interestingly enough, Kashyap began his career as a medical man and later on devoted his entire energy to botany. Although he did valuable research in several branches of botany, his primary interest lay in the vegetable kingdom. His contributions to three areas–the sexual generation of Equisetum, the Liverworts of the Western Himalayas and the Flora of Tibet–are outstanding. One of his very first papers appeared in 1919, in which he described the structure and development of the sexual generation of *Equisetum debile*, one of the Indian members of the family of horsetails growing in Lahore, and his paper was very different from the existing information about the many species that had been discovered by European and American botanists. In 1917, his hypothesis that the sexual generation of other species would show a similar structure to the India species (if certain conditions with regard to space and nourishment were fulfilled) proved to be correct.

The second subject of Kashyap's research was the small group of Liverworts or Hepatica. By identifying and describing four new genera and 30 new species of Liverworts, he contributed a great deal to the knowledge of these species. Professor Goebel of Munich University, one of the leading international botanists of his times, acknowledged the significance of his work in these words, 'You have struck a gold vein in the Western Himalayas and most valuable addition to our knowledge of Liverworts'. His contribution to the Theory of Evolution by reduction regarding this group of plants has also received accolades from scientists throughout the world. Kashyap not only expanded the existing theory, but also placed it on a firm basis by following various lines of evolution. His monograph on the *Liverworts of the Western Himalayas and the*

Punjab Plains filled a great gap in the botanical literature of India. The third subject in which he carried out significant work was the flora of the Western Himalayas and Central Tibet, which he had collected at nine different places throughout its length, and several times at some places. Among the regions he visited are Ladakh, Mountain Kailas and Lake Mansarovar, from where he brought a large collection of plants. Ultimately deposited at Government College, Lahore, these plants formed the nucleus of a large herbarium of hitherto unknown plants. Besides adding to the botanical knowledge of these regions, he even extended their geographical information. In recognition of his sterling contribution, the Panjab University conferred upon him the honoris causa, the degree of Doctor of Science in 1933, the year of its Silver Jubilee celebrations.[44]

Kashyap was one of the founder-members and the first secretary of the Asiatic Society of Bengal. As the first secretary of the Indian Botanical Society (founded in 1920), he did all the spade-work in its organization. He was its President in 1925 and the editor-in-chief of its *Journal of the Indian Botanical Society*. He was also an Advisory Editor of *Chronica Botanica*, published from Holland. He was elected president of the Botany Section of the Indian Science Congress in 1919 at Bombay. In 1934, he was elected a fellow of the Indian Academy of Sciences.[45] Shiv Ram Kashyap, who died in his early 50s, motivated his students to join research. His students Pran Nath Mehra (1907-94)[46] and Amar Chand Joshi (1908-71) became well-known botanists and distinguished administrators. After completing his graduation at Amritsar, P.N. Mehra received his MSc (Honours School) degree in botany from Panjab University, Lahore. Under the influence of Shiv Ram Kashyap, the then head of department of botany and the doyen of Indian bryology, Mehra was awarded the degree of Doctor of Science by the same university. With a brilliant academic career and significant contribution to botanical research, Dr. Mehra was appointed head of the department of botany at Panjab University as early as 1944. After India gained independence in 1947, he continued as head of the department of the New University of Panjab and worked at Khalsa College, Amritsar where the department was temporarily located. Afterwards, when Panjab University shifted to its new campus at Chandigarh, he continued to head the botany department as well as its research wing. Besides, Professor Mehra remained the head of the department of pharmacogonosy and pharmaceutical chemistry at the Panjab University from 1947-60.

Without going into details of the honours and awards won for his contribution to botanical research and scientific knowledge, it may be said that Professor Mehra presented an advanced hypothesis regarding the origin and evolution in hepatics—a 'new condensation theory'. He is well known for his contribution to cytology. Briefly speaking, Professor Mehra, apart from adding to the field of knowledge initiated by his mentor S.R. Kashyap, propounded new theories. Some of these may be mentioned as follows: a 'new condensation theory' on the origin and evolution in hepatics; phyletic classification of ferns which generated a worldwide interest in search of a satisfactory phylogeny of the living ferns; cytological evolution in hardwoods involving the most comprehensive investigation on the forest trees not only in India, but also throughout the world; saturation hypothesis for the absence of polyploidy in conifers; 'Gene block' hypothesis as applied to ferns and flowering plants; authentication of Indian drugs and the identification of details of a large number of indigenous drugs, especially in the Ayurvedic system of medicine.

Amar Chand Joshi,[47] who hailed from Hoshiarpur in Punjab, joined the Government College, Lahore, after passing his FSc (Medical) from the Forman Christian College in the same city. Owing to his keen intellect and interest in angiosperms, he became a favourite of Professor Kashyap, the then head of the department of botany. Joshi joined as a demonstrator at the Panjab University, Lahore, in 1930, and continued until 1931. His monograph entitled *Flora of Lahore,* written at that time, is still consulted by students of botany in Punjab on both sides of the border. He received his DSc in 1937. He had brief stints as assistant professor at the Banaras Hindu University during 1931-34 (where he developed an active school of research on the anatomy of angiosperms), and as an editor of the *Dictionary of*

Economic Products under the Council of Scientific and Industrial Research in 1945. In the same year, he was selected as professor of botany at the Government College, Lahore, and as director of the Panjab University Botanical Laboratory, where he worked up to the partition in 1947. The partition of Punjab created confusion, and educational institutions were dispersed in a number of towns in the province. The new Botanical Laboratory was located at the Government College, Hoshiarpur, where Joshi worked from 1947 to 1951. Without going into the details of his various assignments, it must be recorded that he was the one who built the new campus of Panjab University in Chandigarh. He remained the vice-chancellor of the university from 1957 to 1965.

Shanti Swarup Bhatnagar (1894-1955)[48] made a unique contribution to physical chemistry. Having lost his father Parmeshari Sahai when he was barely eight months old, he was brought up by his maternal grandfather Munshi Pyare Lal, one of the earliest graduates of the Roorkee Engineering College who settled in Sikandarabad (United Provinces). Impressed by his sharp intelligence, his father's friend Raghu Nath Sahai took him under his charge and admitted him to the Dyal Singh High School, Panipat, where he was the headmaster. In 1911, as a schoolboy, his keen interest in scientific experiments resulted in his finding a substitute for carbon electrodes, which could not be imported. Bhatnagar was pushed to revive his interest in the problem which had provoked his curiosity as a schoolboy. His brief interaction with Professor N.N. Godbole as an Intermediate student in the recently opened Dyal Singh College drew his attention to the industrial potential of indigenous fruits. It resulted in the publication of Bhatnagar's article. 'Fermentation Phenomenon of Pomegranate Juice', in the magazine *Raushani* ('Light'), the organ of the Society for Promoting Scientific Knowledge, launched by the Lahore Medical College students. In 1913, he joined the BSc course in the Forman Christian College and earned his degree in 1916. While working as a student-demonstrator in physics and chemistry in the local Dyal Singh College and later as senior demonstrator at the Forman Christian College, he studied for his MSc course and earned the degree in 1918.

Among the teachers he remembered with gratitude were Mr. Welinker, Principal of Dyal Singh College (later Director of Public Instruction), Professor B.M. Jones, later vice-chancellor, Leeds University, Professor B.K. Singh and Ruchi Ram Sahni. The latter was largely responsible for awarding a scholarship from the Dyal Singh College Trust for Bhatnagar's studies abroad. After two years of work in the Ramsay Laboratories, he submitted his thesis, titled 'Solubilities of bi-trivalent salts of higher fatty acids in oils and their effect on the surface tension of oils', under the supervision of Professor F.G. Donovan, FRS of University College, London University. He earned his DSc degree in 1921. During the period of research, he received a fellowship to the amount of 250 from the Directorate of Scientific and Industrial Research (DSIR) of Great Britain. After his return in August 1921, Bhatnagar was appointed professor of chemistry in the newly established Banaras Hindu University, where he created an active School of Physico-Chemical Research within three years of his stay.

The most significant period of his career began in 1924, when he was appointed University Professor of Physical-Chemistry and Director of Panjab University Chemical Laboratories; he was later elected Dean of University Instruction. The 16 years from 1924-40 were the most fruitful in terms of his scientific contribution. Apart from being a very inspiring teacher, he was a great experimenter and a gifted writer. The major fields of his study were colloid chemistry and magneto-chemistry. However, his research work in applied and industrial chemistry proved to be of great practical value, as was evident from his solution of the mud problem which appeared intractable for Messrs Steel Brothers and Company of London. Its representative, the Attock Oil Company, faced this problem while drilling oil in Rawalpindi. Bhatnagar solved this problem by adding an Indian gum, which lowered the viscosity of the mud suspension and added to its stability against the fluctuating tendency of electrolytes. Instead of accepting a sum of Rs 1,50,000 offered to him for his research work on petroleum-related subjects, Bhatnagar asked the company to give it to the university. Later, this amount was increased, and the duration of the research project extended from five to 10 years. A unit was launched as a department of petroleum research under his guidance. Six research scholars were engaged under this scheme, and scholarships named after five eminent men of Punjab and Professor Donovan of London University, where Bhatnagar had worked for his DSc. This research project resulted in an exploration of a number of related problems, namely deodorisation of waxes, increasing the flame-height of kerosene, lubrication, prevention of corrosion, and utilization of waste products in the vegetable oil and mineral industries. The results of this research project proved to be of great industrial value. Bhatnagar offered 50 per cent of all income from patents to the university, which was to be utilised for scientific research. Bhatnagar's persistent refusal to accept financial rewards for himself can be explained by his conviction that 'scientific work would lose its altruistic and truly cultural character if the worker becomes money-minded and begins to secure financial benefits for himself'. While delivering the Convocation address to the Panjab University in 1936, Tej Bahadur Sapru acknowledged his generosity in the following words :

> [T]hat he had with a singular sense of patriotism and self-denial transmitted a considerable part of that gift [offered by Messrs Steel Brother & Co., London] to the Chemistry Department of your University, so as to create an Industrial Research Department, in which some research scholars could develop new processes for the industrial utilisation of Indian raw materials, I felt that your University was lucky in possessing a Professor who was alive to his duty to the country.

Indeed, nationalistic feelings imbued Bhatnagar with so much courage that he touched the feet of the Congress president on the latter's release from jail in 1940, despite his knighthood and official position as director (since re-designated as director-general) of the Council of Scientific and Industrial Research.

The year 1940 disrupted his relationship with Panjab University as the British Government appointed Bhatnagar the director of the Board of Scientific and Industrial Research. Established to produce essential items for British soldiers fighting in World War II, it was renamed the Council of Scientific and Industrial Research. In spite of heavy administrative duties, Bhatnagar continued his research work and developed several patents of great importance with the help of his staff. Most of these patents related to items required for the war effort : anti-gas cloth and varnish air-foam solution, vegetable oil blends as lubricants and fuels, unburstable containers, glass substitutes, dehydrated castor oil, and plastic from Indian wastes. As director of scientific and industrial research, Dr Bhatnagar had to serve under several members of the Viceroy's Executive Council, namely Sir A. Ramaswamy Mudaliar, Sir Azizul Haque, Sir Ardeshir Dalal. When India became a sovereign democratic republic, he worked under C. Rajagopalachari and ultimately under Prime Minister Jawaharlal Nehru, who took an active interest in the development of science and technology. During the period of active teaching and research at the Banaras Hindu University and Panjab University, Lahore, Bhatnagar inspired a large number of students and collaborators who distinguished themselves as teachers and researchers. Among them were Mata Prasad (Principal, Royal Institute of Science and later Director, Central Research Institute and Vice-Chancellor, Vikram University), S.S. Joshi (Professor of Chemistry and Principal, College of Science, Banaras University), D.L. Srivastava (Deputy-Director, Central Drug Research Institute, Lucknow), K.N. Mathur (Deputy-Director, National Physical Laboratory, Delhi and later Director, Scientific Instruments Organisation), B.D. Jain (Professor of Inorganic Chemistry, Delhi University), Balwant Singh (Professor, Government College, Ludhiana), T.N. Seth (Professor of Biochemistry, Medical College, Patna), and Professor Bashir Ahmad (Director, University Institute of Chemistry, Lahore and later Vice-Chancellor).

To sum up his achievements, it might be said that Bhatnagar was interested not only in pure science, but also in its practical utilisation. On the organisational side, he accomplished a pioneering work such as the establishment of the National Research Development Corporation, which acted as a bridge between research and development. Last, but not least, was his significant role as initiator of the Industrial Association

Movement in India. The British Government bestowed a number of awards and honours upon Dr. Bhatnagar in appreciation of his multifaceted scientific contributions. In 1936, the British Government conferred the OBE upon him for his excellent work in pure and applied chemistry. For his contribution to the war effort, he was knighted in 1941. In 1943, the Society of Chemicals Industry, London, elected him an honorary member and later Vice-President. In the same year, he was elected Fellow of the Royal Society, London. He was awarded the Padma Vibhushan by the President of India.

Fondly remembered as the 'poet of Mathematics' by his associates, Sarvadaman Chawla (1907-45) made a substantial contribution to the advancement of Number Theory, a branch of mathematics that deals with the subtle laws and relationships that govern numbers. Encouraged by his parents–Gopal Singh Chawla and Shakuntala—the junior Chawla worked hard to develop his keen aptitude for numbers. Just after receiving his Master's degree in 1928 from Panjab University, he presented three papers, '[17], [21], [24]', at the Conference of the Indian Mathematical Society in December, where his father, too, presented his paper 'Landens' Transformation'. In 1931, he submitted his doctoral thesis titled 'Contributions to Analytic Theory of Numbers'. An alumnus of Panjab University, he was one of the three winners of the Ramanujan Memorial Prize, awarded by the University of Madras for the best original thesis in Mathematics. Before he joined as Professor-in-Mathematics at the Government College of Lahore in 1936, he worked briefly as a lecturer at St. Stephen's College, Delhi (1931), and Banaras Hindu University (1932), and as reader and head at Andhra University in Waltair (1932-35), where he was invited by Dr. S. Radhakrishnan. He joined as professor of mathematics at the Government College, Lahore, in 1936, where his father had held the same position almost a decade ago. During the course of his tenures at these universities, Chawla made a creative impact on Mathematics and on his colleagues in the field.[49] According to C.S. Rao and Professor R.P. Bambah (ex Vice-Chancellor, Panjab University, Chandigarh, 1985-95) he drew many students to research.[50] Dr. Bambah was one of them. The Nobel laureate Abdus Salam was also his student.

Chawla's original contribution to the advancement of knowledge in mathematics, particularly the Number Theory, has been celebrated by his students in India and Pakistan. According to Herman Weyle, 'Every one of his researches contains interesting observations, and most of them give their subjects a new turn by introducing original ideas. Sometimes they are devoted to simplified proofs of difficult classical problems, but more often they give new results, not seldom of a quite surprising character.'[51] Besides making significant contributions to Analytical and Algebraic Number Theory, he made valuable additions to elliptic integrals and functions, Elementary Number Theory, Ramanujan's function, partitions, character sums, the Rieman Zeta function and Dirichlets L-functions, Diophantine equations and inequalities, as well as combinatorics. Sarvadaman Chawla is best known to the mathematical community for four theorems which bear his name: the Ankeny-Artin-Chowla theorem, the Bruck-Chowla-Ryser Theorem, the Chowla-Mordell theorem, and the Chowla-Selberg formula. For S. Chawla, mathematics was something to be shared freely. Commenting on this aspect of his stimulating professional relationship, R.P. Bambah (his erstwhile student at the Government College, Lahore), remarked, 'Even when he [Chawla] was successfully working on important results, he would let others join in. He wrote more than 300 papers and collaborated with more than sixty co-authors.'[52] During the course of his career in India, Chawla wrote joint papers with Indian mathematicians K. Ananda Rao, S.S. Pillai, S. Sastry, H. Gupta, A.M. Mian, R.C. Bose, C.R. Rao, D. Singh, A.R. Nazir, T. Vijayaraghvan, R.P. Bambah and F.C. Auluck. His foreign collaborators included distinguished American scholars such as Atle Selberg, Paul Erdos, L.J. Mordell, H. Davenport, E. Artin, Richard Brauer, N.C. Ankeny, P.T. Bateman, G. Shimura, H.J. Ryser, I.N. Herstein, Don Lewis, H. Harse, B.W. Jones, T.M. Apostol, E. Strauss, H.B. Mann, B.J. Birch, Marshall Hall Jr., A. Borel, R. Ayoub, H. Zassenhaus, B.C. Brandt, K. Ramchandra, and many others. It may be added that he guided more than 18 Ph.D. theses in the USA.[53]

A renowned experimental physicist, Pratap Krishan

Kitchlew (1899-1982)[54] passed his matriculation in 1917, did his BSc in physics in 1921, and MSc in physics from Panjab University. Under the supervision of Meghnad Saha, he received his DSc degree from Allahabad University in 1927, and then joined Patna University. In 1929, Kitchlew moved over to the physics department in the Panjab University; and in due course of time became a professor and joined Delhi University in the early part of 1947. In 1930, Meghnad Saha took Kitchlew along with him for a tour of the renowned centres of learning in Europe and England. It was a valuable learning experience, which revealed to him the urgency of self-reliance, especially in scientific and industrial instruments and components for India. In pursuit of his new insight and conviction, he undertook development projects under the research programme of the Council of Scientific and Industrial Research. However, his well-documented reports were assigned to cold storage. In the meantime, he engaged himself in the research and design of applied optics called spectroscopy. It is in this area that he made his major contribution. As a teacher and researcher at the Panjab University, Kitchlew devoted all his energy to developing scientific techniques for finding multiple axes of 'Diamond Crystals' for industrial purposes. These experiments were conducted in his personal laboratory, which contained a network of glass apparatus for studying phenomena connected with electrical discharge through nitrogen. Dr. Harshvardhan, Director of the Central Scientific Instruments Organisation, Chandigarh, recalled, 'The Department of Physics of Panjab University, Lahore was smoothly run, dedicated and well-respected for teaching, training and applied research in physics'.[55] His students, namely Narinder Singh Bhalla, Ved Prakash Puri, Inder Sen Kapur and Mohinder Prakash Puri, owed their lifelong devotion to physics to Professor Kitchlew's rigorous training during their time as his assistants in a number of scientific projects. Working with his assistants, Kitchlew developed the techniques of making quartz micro-balance, X-ray tubes, photoflash bulbs, diamond tools and diamond working machines, synthetic sapphires, vacuum furnaces, calcium fluoride crystals, vacuum units, etc., and many other items through various research schemes. The technique-oriented training imparted to so many students is 'an example of foresight and his unique contribution to the growth of technology at a time when few were even conscious of this need'.

A significant turn occurred in his professional career just before the partition riots, when Kitchlew joined as professor in physics at Delhi University. To put it briefly, his dynamic personality spruced up the physics workshop in order to continue his work on diamond X-ray patterns. His student Harshvardhan joined him sometime later as his assistant to work on obtaining patterns of diamond crystals. It may be mentioned that many colleges in Delhi had been affiliated to the Panjab University until 1922–the year that Delhi University came into existence. By the time Kitchlew retired in 1962 from Delhi University, his work on spectroscopy had entered its finest phase. Despite being invited to join as the director of the National Physical Laboratory in October 1963, he left it in September 1964 owing to his differences over the patterns and style of administration in science. Ultimately, he devoted himself to his factory for designing and manufacturing optical components, and in a short time his factory became the Adam Hilger of India, like the one in the UK. In recognition of his lifelong work and lasting contributions to the field of industrial and applied optics, Kitchlew was awarded the Meghnad Saha Memorial Medal by the Asiatic Society in 1980.

Among other notable scientists who were also alumni of the Panjab University, Lahore, but did not have a long stint as either teachers or researchers were Piara Singh Gill, Sunder Singh Hora and Karm Narayan Behl. However, I shall focus only on Piara Singh Gill (1911-2002), whose association with the university was the longest. Coming from the village of Chela in Hoshiarpur, he matriculated from the Khalsa High School, Mahilpur (Hoshiarpur), in 1928. The political trials and tribulations of his elder brother, who was arrested by the British Government for his participation in the national movement, led him to leave his enslaved country and study abroad in an atmosphere of freedom. Overcoming all obstacles, he reached the USA and worked hard to earn money for his education. Piara Singh secured his BSc and MA (in physics and mathematics) degrees in 1935 and 1936 respectively at the University of California, where he earned a tuition scholarship for his studies. Beginning his research career in 1937 under the famous American physics Nobel laureate Arthur Holy Compton, Piara Singh did extremely good work on Time-Variation of Cosmic Rays. His doctoral dissertation on *Further Studies of Cosmic Rays on the Pacific Ocean* established the latitude effect of Cosmic Rays at sea level after accounting for the temperature effect. The *New York Times* reported his work and that of his associate Marcel Schein in its issue dated June 30, 1939. In March 1940, he received his doctorate degree in physics at the 199th convocation of the University of Chicago.

After his return to India on a travelling fellowship (1940-41), Piara Singh Gill carried out experiments on the Azimuthal Variation of Cosmic-rays, which could be conducted at the latitudes and attitudes available in India. He became a lecturer in physics at Forman Christian College, Lahore (1940-47). Despite the fact that research was not regarded as a lucrative career, Gill inspired a number of young students to pursue it. Sometime in 1947 he moved to the Tata Institute of Fundamental Research, Bombay, where H.J. Bhabha was director. He reached the peak of his career at Aligarh University, where he was invited to be professor of physics by Jawaharlal Nehru, then Prime Minister of India. At this university, studies on the development of G.M. Counters, Neutron Counters, Nuclear Emulsion technique, and sophisticated electronic circuit for various experiments were completed successfully under his guidance.

IV

Conclusion

A review of the development of modern sciences at the Panjab University during India's pre-independence period highlight three crucial issues: the nature and goals of the introduction, development and diffusion of Western sciences through higher educational institutions; the response of Indian scientists with regard to the tension between the cultivation of Western science and the demands of the ongoing national struggle for freedom; and the conflict between the colonial agenda and the needs and aspirations of the Indian people.

The first issue concerning the nature and goals of the introduction, development and diffusion of Western sciences through higher educational institutions has to be explained with reference to the colonial project, which had set its sights on augmenting the capacity of the mother country to feed its ongoing industrial revolution by exploiting the human and material resources of the colonised country. The establishment of as many as 170 colleges, including several medical and engineering institutions (affiliated to the five Universities of Calcutta, Madras, Bombay, Lahore and Delhi), and 10 scientific services had only trained and employed Indians as clerks, second-rank technicians, and engineers to run railways, shipping or canal construction ventures, or gather information about botanical, zoological and mineral resources.[56] Transfer and relocation of Western scientific knowledge and technologies were only partly successful in terms of their long-term benefits for the Indian people. This was because these ventures were conceived of as, and remained, mere technological projects that did not target the development and diffusion of knowledge and skills. Indians were educated only up to a certain point, and the culture of technology was withheld from them.[57] As colonial subjects, non-Europeans including Indians were deliberately denied opportunities for enterprise, investment and experience. This is evident from Rai Bahadur Ganga Ram's experience, who was discouraged not only from making an investment in lift-irrigation technology to harness water near Renala in Lower Bari Doab Canal, but also deprived of contracts to construct tube-wells on his plot in Upper Chenab Colony (now in west Punjab, Pakistan).[58]

The second issue, which concerned the response of the Indian scientists, requires a closer look at the tension between the desire (and compulsion) for the acquisition and cultivation of Western scientific knowledge, and the demands of nationalistic urges. Indian scientists viewed this issue from a complex perspective. For example, Jagadish Chandra Bose, with his firm belief in the Brahmo-inspired universalism, argued that knowledge was not the monopoly of any race, and thus '... science is neither of the East nor of West but international'. The majority of Indian scientists sincerely believed that unity and universality were crucial to the growth of civilisation and the common heritage of mankind. However, their bitter experiences as colonial subjects obliged them to confront the cultural chauvinism of British imperialists, who claimed scientific genius and achievements as the prerogative of the Anglo-Saxon races and behaved arrogantly. For example, Professor B.M. Jones, head of the chemistry department, Government College of Lahore, became quite envious of the popularity that Ruchi Ram Sahni enjoyed, and tried to insult him at the slightest pretext. In his memoirs, *Self-Revelations of an Octogenarian*, Ruchi Ram Sahni has written about the blatant racial discrimination Indians faced in matters of recruitment and promotion in professional institutions, administrative and scientific services, as well as in daily life.

Despite the wilful denial of opportunities for professional growth and promotion by the colonial state, the nationalist-minded Indian scientists did not boycott either colleges, universities, scientific institutions, or honorific titles. They channelled their frustration and anger into more creative avenues, among which can be counted the creation of scientific awareness among Indians living in urban and rural areas, thereby improving the quality of science teaching in schools, the establishment of institutes/associations for the cultivation of science, the opening of Swadeshi chemical industries and scientific workshops, the translation of Western scientific works into vernacular languages, advanced research in mathematics, botany, zoology, physics and chemistry in foreign universities as preparation for national service in independent India, and the training of students and guiding them in research on topics chosen from the global basket.

The third issue concerns the conflict between the agenda of colonial science and the needs and aspirations of the Indian people. Colonial rulers perceived three potential roles for science. The first was concerned with exploration and discovery, the second with environmental and disease problems, and the third with providing ongoing advice and technical services. All these roles were targeted at exploiting the colonies' potential in terms of their human and natural resources, as a tribute exacted from hapless colonial subjects. Neither the development of the intellectual potential of the subject people nor the economic modernisation of their country was on the agenda of the British rulers, who increasingly harnessed science and technology to bolster the empire and capitalism. It was not only scientific education that was underdeveloped but research, too, as is evident from the fact that the Panjab University, whose finances as well as academic and infrastructure development were under the tight control of the British Government, took more than three decades after its inception to establish departments of physics, chemistry, and other sciences. Historically speaking, the development of science and technology was a colonial instrument to aid social control and economic exploitation with a view to perpetuating political hegemony in India. The Indian intelligentsia, including scientists, historians, literati and political ideologues-cum-activists of all hues resisted successfully and set their own terms of dialogue. The self-assured scientist directly or indirectly articulated his nationalist urges and recovered his agency, which was constantly being negotiated under the burden of colonialism in the first two phases: autodidact (self-teaching and translation activity) and renaissance.

REFERENCES

1. Shiv Visvanathan, *Organising for Science*, p. 8.
2. Letter No. 296, dated June 10, 1865, from the Secretary, Panjab Government, to the Director of Public Instruction, Panjab. Cited in J.F. Bruce, *A History of the University of Panjab*, p. 11. It was consulted in the Library of Government College, Lahore.
3. *Report of the Anjuman-i-Panjab*, 1867-68, Part I, p. 18.
4. *Panjab Government Proceedings*, November 1868 (Education), p. 9. Cited in Bruce, *A History of the University of Panjab*, p. 20.
5. Bruce, *A History of the University of Punjab*, p. 23.

6. For the preceding account regarding the unique features of the Panjab University, see *Punjab Government Educational Report,* 1883, p. 26; Sir Alfred Craft, *Review of Education in India,* 1886; *Punjab Government Gazette*– Act XIX of 1882; this was an Act to establish and incorporate the University of Panjab; Punjab Archives, Lahore.
7. *Punjab Government Educational Report, 1883-84,* Report of the Director of Public Instruction, Punjab Archives, Lahore.
8. I have based my account of the various appointments in science subjects on H.L.O. Garrett and Abdul Hamid, *A History of Government College, Lahore, 1864-1964* (it originally covered the period 1864-1914 and was printed in 1914; both editions are available in the College Library); *A History of Gazetted Officers,* Punjab Civil List.
9. James G. Huard and Kenneth S. Williams (eds), *The Collected Papers of Sarvadaman Chowla,* pp. iii-iv. These papers were obtained through courtesy of Professor R.P. Bambah.
10. Ibid., p. iv.
11. Garrett and Hamid, *A History of Government College, Lahore.*
12. *History of Gazetted Officers,* Punjab Civil List, 1900, p. 110.
13. Garrett and Hamid, *A History of Government College, Lahore,* p. 110.
14. *History of Gazetted Officers,* Punjab Civil List, 1900, p. 607.
15. Garrett and Hamid, *A History of Government College, Lahore,* pp. 113, 141.
16. Information in the two paragraphs is drawn from Ibid., pp. 109, 123, 128-9 and 178.
17. Ibid., p. 129.
18. Ibid.
19. Ibid., p. 131.
20. Ibid., p. 136.
21. Bruce, *A History of the University of Panjab,* pp. 137-8.
22. *Birbal Sahni* (1891-1949): The illustrious son of Ruchi Ram Sahni was a student of the Government College, Lahore. Deeply influenced by his teacher Professor Shiv Ram Kashyap, he decided to become a botanist. After his graduation in 1911 from Panjab University, he completed his Tripos in natural sciences from Cambridge. Under the inspiring guidance of Professor Albert Charles Seward, an internationally acclaimed palaeobotanist, Birbal Sahni worked for his research. In 1919, he was awarded the degree of DSc by the London University for his thesis on fossil plants. While still a student at Cambridge, Sahni was asked to revise Lawson's textbook of botany to suit

the requirements of students of botany in India. *The Textbook of Botany* by Lawson and Sahni became a widely read book, both in the colleges and universities of India. For almost a year, he worked as professor of botany at the Banaras Hindu University and the Panjab University. Soon after, he joined the newly opened department of botany in Lucknow University and served there till his death in 1949. Along with his colleagues, he founded an Institute of Palaeobotany on September 10, 1946.

The preceding profile is based on a pamphlet, *Professor Birbal Sahni,* Lucknow: Birbal Sahni Institute of Palaeobotany, 2002, pp. 1–13.

23. *Panjab University Calendar,* 1921-22, pp. 544-5.
24. Bruce, *A History of the University of Panjab,* p. 154.
25. R.R. Sethi and J.L. Mehta, *A History of the Panjab University, Chandigarh, 1947-1967,* p. 25; Bruce, *A History of the University of Panjab,* p. 163.
26. Ibid., p. 26.
27. Bruce, *A History of the University of Panjab,* p. 148.
28. Garrett and Hamid, *A History of Government College, Lahore,* p. 206.
29. The discussion in this paragraph is based on ibid., pp. 206-7.
30. *Panjab University Calendar,* 1935-36, Vol. II, p. 441.
31. Ibid., p. 443.
32. *Panjab University Calendar,* 1937-38, Vol. II, p. 467.
33. *Panjab University Calendar,* 1941-42, Part II, p. 812.
34. Sethi and Mehta, *A History of the Panjab University,* p.34.
35. Cited in Narender K. Sehgal and Subodh Mahanti (eds), *Memoirs of Ruchi Ram Sahni: Pioneer of Science Popularisation in Punjab,* p. xxvii.
36. Ibid., pp. 17-9.
37. Ruchi Ram Sahni, *Self-Revelations of an Octogenarian,* p. 11. The typed manuscript is lying with his grandson, Professor Ashok Sahni, Panjab University, Chandigarh.
38. Regarding the significance of his Calcutta experience, see Kamlesh Mohan, 'Ruchi Ram Sahni and the Pursuit of Science in a Colonial Society', p. 115.
39. Ibid., p. 116.
40. Ibid., p. 117.
41. Ibid., p. 118.
42. Shan Muhammad, ed., *Writings and Speeches of Sir Syed Ahmed Khan,* pp. 231-2.
43. Kamlesh Mohan, 'Ruchi Ram Sahni', p. 118. Both Munshi Zakaullah, a student of Master Ramchandra in Delhi, and Akshay Kumar Dutt in Calcutta, had shown an acute awareness

of and concern with the consequences of English education, especially its role in alienating young students from their own national culture.

44. My account of Shiv Ram Kashyap's life, professional career, and his contribution to botanical knowledge and literature is based on H. Chaudhri, 'Obituary Notice': N.B.D., 'Tribute to an Indian Botanist': and Shiv Ram Kashyap, 'An Account of a Journey to the Gangotri Glacier'. I obtained these documents from his daughter Uma Sood, alias Kamini Kaushal, the famous actress.
45. Ibid.
46. My analysis of Pran Nath Mehra's life, career and achievements as a botanist is based on the *Biographical Memoirs Series,* pp. 11-33. He was elected as a Fellow in 1952.
47. Ibid., pp. 130-42. He was elected as a Fellow in 1938.
48. My analysis of Shanti Swarup Bhatnagar's life, career and achievements is based on the *Biographical Memoirs Series,* pp. 32-48. He had been a foundation Fellow since 1935. Norah Richards, *Sir Shanti Swarup Bhatnagar FRS: A Biographical Study of India's Eminent Scientist.*
49. James G. Huard, 'Sarvadaman Chowla (1907-1995)', pp. iii-vi.
50. Interview with Professor R.P. Bambah on October 16, 2007. M. Ram Murty, et al., 'The Work of Sarvadaman Chowla', p. vii; C.S. Rao in Ibid., p. xxi.
51. M. Ram Murty, et al., 'The Work of Sarvadaman Chowla', p. vi.
52. R.P. Bambah, 'Sarvadaman Chowla (1907-1993)' pp. 105-6. Presented on his 75th birthday at the International Conference on Number Theory and Discrete Mathematics in honour of Srinivas Ramanujan (1887-1920), Chandigarh, October 2000. It was published in the *Biographical Memoirs Series.*
53. Ibid., p. 107.
54. I have based my account of the life, career and contribution of Pratap Krishan Kitchlew on the *Biographical Memoirs Series,* pp. 35-47. He was the Foundation Fellow; interviews with his students, namely Drs. J.N. Nanda, P.M. Sood and Raj Kumar Verma.
55. Cited in Ibid., p. 37.
56. R.M. MacLeod, 'Scientific Advice for British India: Imperial Perception and Administrative Goals, 1898-1923' in *Modern Asian Studies,* 9(3), 1975.
57. Ian Inkster, 'Prometheus Bound: Technology and Industrialisation in Japan, China and India Prior to 1914: A Political Economy Approach', in *Annals of Science*, 45, 1988.
58. Imran Ali, *The Punjab Under Imperialism, 1885-1947*, pp. 218-22.

BIBLIOGRAPHY

Archival Sources

Sahni, Ruchi Ram, *Self-Revelations of an Octogenarian*, Typed manuscript in possession of Professor Ashok Sahni, Panjab University, Chandigarh.

Kashyap, Shiv Ram, 'An Account of a Journey to the Gangotri Glacier', Reprint No. 20 from *Urusvati Journal* (New York: Urusvati Himalayan Research Institute of Roerich Museum).

Secondary Sources

A History of Gazetted Officers, Punjab Civil List, 1900.

Ali, Imran, 1989, *The Punjab Under Imperialism, 1885-1947* (Delhi: Oxford University Press).

Bambah, R.P., 2000, 'Sarvadaman Chowla (1907-1993)', in *Collected Papers of R.P. Bambah*

(Chandigarh: Centre for Advanced Study in Mathematics).

Biographical Memoirs Series, n.d. (New Delhi: Indian National Science Academy).

Bruce, J.F., 1933, *A History of the University of Panjab* (Lahore).

Chaudhri, H., 1937, 'Obituary Notice', *Proceedings of the Indian Academy of Sciences*, V (6), Sec. B.

Craft, Alfred, 1886, Review of Education in India.

Garret, H.L.O. and Abdul Hamid, 1964, *A History of Government College, Lahore, 1864-1964* (Lahore).

Huard, James G., 1999, 'Sarvadamam Chowla (1907-1995)', in James G. Huard and Kenneth S. Willians (eds), *The Collected Papers of Sarvadaman Chowla* (Carleton: University of Carleton).

Huard, James G. and Kenneth S. Williams (eds), 1999, *The Collected Papers of Sarvadaman Chowla* (Carleton: University of Carleton).

Inkster, Ian, 1988, 'Prometheus Bound: Technology and Industrialisation in Japan, China and India Prior to 1914: A Political Economy Approach', *Annals of Science*, 45.

MacLeod, R.M., 1975, 'Scientific Advice for British India: Imperial Perception and Administrative Goals, 1898-1923', *Modern Asian Studies*, 9 (3).

Mahanti, Subodh, and Narender K. Sehgal (eds), 1994, *Memoirs of Ruchi Ram Sahni: Pioneer of Science Popularisation in Punjab* (New Delhi: Vigyan Prasar).

Mehta, J.L. and R.R. Sethi, 1968, *A History of the Panjab University, Chandigarh, 1947-1967* (Chandigarh: Panjab University Publication Bureau).

Mohan, Kamlesh, 2000, 'Ruchi Ram Sahni and the Pursuit of Science in a Colonial Society', in Narender K. Sehgal, Satpal Sangwan and Subodh Mahanti (eds), *Uncharted Terrains: Essays on Science Popularisation in Pre-Independence India* (New Delhi: Vigyan Prasar).

Muhammad, Shan (ed.), 1972, *Writings and Speeches of Sir Syed Ahmed Khan* (Bombay: Asia Publishing House).

Murty, V. Kumar, M. Ram Murty and Kenneth S. Williams, 1999, 'The Work of Sarvadaman Chowla', in James G. Huard and Kenneth S. Williams (eds), *The Collected Papers of Sarvadaman Chowla* (Carleton: University of Carleton).

N.B.D., 1982, 'Tribute to an Indian Botanist', *Illustrated Weekly*, 31 October.

Panjab University Calendar, 1935-36, 1937-38, 1941-42.

Professor Birbal Sahni (Lucknow: Birbal Sahni Institute of Palaeobotany, 2002).

Report of the Anjuman-i-Panjab, 1867-68.

Richards, Norah, 2004 [1948] *Sir Shanti Swarup Bhatnagar FRS: A Biographical Study of India's Eminent Scientist* (Lahore; Reprint, New Delhi: National Institute of Science, Technology and Development Studies).

Visvanathan, Shiv, 1985, *Organising for Science: The Making of an Industrial Research Laboratory* (Delhi: Oxford University Press).

3

Technology and Religion

Recasting Hindu Consciousness Through Print in India with Special Reference to the Punjab During the Nineteenth Century

The three inventions that the English philosopher Francis Bacon identified as the source of great changes in the European Renaissance— printing, gunpowder and magnetic compass— were the products of the East specifically Chinese and not European civilisation. In his view, this triumvirate played a major role in revolutionising warfare and navigation.[1] I would add human consciousness to this list. In this paper, I shall try to discuss the gradually evolving relationship between print technology and religion, with special reference to its impact on Hindu consciousness. Their close interaction had its beginning in Bengal during the Brahmo Samaj phase but matured with the birth and expansion of the Arya Samaj. This paper focuses on the region of Punjab excluding the Princely States.

The relationship between religion and technology is two-fold. On the one hand, cultural values particularly religious may intervene in the choice and actual use of technology. On the other hand, technology once adopted may affect different aspects of social relations and world-view. It may be used as an instrument to shape human consciousness and its responses. Gutenberg's moveable typeset accelerated the revolution in this area. This is, of course, the remarkable insight of Marshall McLuhan and George Steiner, who perceive a significant transformation of human consciousness as it moves from oral to written word and from the domination by sound to domination by visual space. Obviously, the change in the modes of acquiring knowledge and disseminating it made a great difference. Knowledge became impersonal, more abstract and intellectual[2]. Nevertheless, its availability to a larger number of people through print technology enabled them to use various methods and techniques to organise their life and resources in a better way as well as to articulate their social, religious and political anxieties or concerns.

The major argument in this paper is that print technology played an important role in transforming the Hindu consciousness of religion from a fuzzy awareness of sharing one God or pantheon to a belief in the fixed scriptural identity and a community of interests whether social, political or economic, on the basis of religion. It was used and continues to be used as a powerful instrument in the hands of the politico-religious leaders to communicate with a large number of people either for popularising radical ideas or for reinforcing revivalist beliefs, values and practices.

In this context, it is important to find out how and why the print technology was acquired, adapted and used by the ideologues and crusaders of the Arya Samaj to implement their reform agenda. For this purpose, I shall divide this discussion into four parts: I. Barriers in the early development of print technology; II. Socialisation of press and its diffusion in the colonial Punjab; III. Swami Dayanand's response to Western science and technologies; IV. Recasting Hindu consciousness through print; V. Conclusion.

I

Barriers in the Early Development of Print Technology

In India, the problem of indifference coupled with resistance to the adoption of print technology in the pre-colonial period had hindered the process of knowledge revolution which occurred in Europe in two stages: paper manufacturing and book printing. Indian artisans and craftsmen had acquired a good deal of skill in technology of paper-making as is evident form Alberuni's references to its use by the Muslims in the earlier part of the eleventh century while Indians specifically Hindus were still writing on palm leaves and bark[3]. In the Sultanate period, Delhi and Lahore were important centres of paper making. Under Sultan Zain-ul-Abedin (AD 1417-67) of Kashmir, an excellent quality of paper was not only produced but also sent as a valuable present to the contemporary Kings, particularly, the rulers of Samarqand[4]. With the rapid diffusion of technical knowledge and ever growing demand for paper as a writing material, paper-making centres were established in Sialkot (Punjab), Zafarabad (Oudh), Bihar Sharif and Arwal (Bihar), Murshidabad and Hooghly (Bengal), Ahmedabad, Khambayat and Pattan (Gujarat), Aurangabad and Mysore (the South)[5]. Besides, Indians had possessed skill in block-printing since the seventh century as is evident from its utilisation by the Buddhist priests to impose Buddha's image on silk and paper. This fact is of special significance in view of the Chinese use of Indian technology for producing books through wood-block printing[6]. Despite the presence of both the technology and skilled manpower in India, the knowledge revolution could not go beyond the first stage, i.e. paper-making.

Indian scholars were presumably familiar with the printed Chinese books owing to frequent contacts between their country and China. They were also exposed to its actual use in Goa when the printing press was first introduced as early as on September 6, 1556 with a view "to release the potential educative value of Christian literature in Indian languages"[7]. In north India, the Mughal rulers had many opportunities to use printed books. While the three Jesuit Missions (1580-1595) presented Akbar with seven volumes of Plantin's Polygot Bible (printed in five languages), the Portuguese had given a printing press as a gift to Jahangir[8]. Both the rulers had shown no interest in promoting the use of print-technology either for circulation of scientific information and techniques among the people for solving their day-to-day problems or for further development of knowledge.

In this context, an important question arises: Why did medieval society in India fail to graduate from paper-manufacture and manuscript copying to book printing despite the availability of technology and skilled manpower? A partial answer can be found in this brief reference to the development of book printing in China. Firstly, experiments with print technology and its growth was primarily facilitated by the policies of the Chinese emperors who were keen to create a class of professional administrators for solving routine problems of governance. In the absence of the tradition of recruitment for jobs in the royal service through a system of rigorous examination, rulers in medieval India could not develop a class of professional administrators. It can be attributed to a highly individualistic and personalised approach to education in *madrassas* which discouraged the development of knowledge and its application by the artisans and craftsmen. Non-existence of appropriate infrastructure coupled with the resultant socio-cultural ethos militated against laying a sound basis for an institutionalised approach to the development of new knowledge and technologies[9].

Secondly, the Mughal rulers failed to create a stimulating social environment for innovation or adoption and expansion of the printing press. Irfan Habib's insightful article has drawn our attention to their ostentatious manners, dresses and interior decorations. He has underlined the adverse consequences of their consumption-oriented outlook for the development of new technologies as well as for the accumulation of knowledge and wisdom[10]. For example, the Indian invention of water-cooling through saltpetre was superior to the contemporary European techniques of refrigeration, especially, in its freedom from use of snow. The technique of making rose-water essence was also discovered by the Empress Nur Jahan. Like the Muslims, the Hindus, too, adopted military technology, fads and fashions with enthusiasm as it was motivated by their security needs and craze for novelty. However, doubts and reluctance characterised their initial response to new things from the West.

Thirdly, the delayed Indian response to printing was influenced by ideological and cultural factors. While analysing the Muslim response to it, Francis Robinson has attributed it to their fundamental scepticism of the written word. He has argued that person to person transmission was at the heart of the transmission of Islamic knowledge. The best way of getting at knowledge was to listen to the author himself[11]. Like in all oral cultures, their distrust of the printed word was linked with their faith in the speaker/prophet. Hence, Muslims regarded the Quran as the divine word. In the beginning, the conservative *ulemas* used it as an argument against printing the Quran.[12] In their view, its availability would reduce the dependence of the disciples on the teacher and thus weaken the priestly authority.

Fourthly, calligraphy (literally meaning transcribing books and royal orders on palm leaves or paper), which was developed as the highest of Islamic arts for embellishing the written text as well as its margins, itself became an inhibiting factor in the adoption of print technology. Being at an initial stage of development, print technology could not satisfy the aesthetic requirements of the Muslim scholars.[13] Resistance and reluctance of *katibs* or scribes could be one factor but it could not have been decisive because they were not yet organised as a class.

Fifthly, the reluctant Indian, especially, Hindu response to the adoption of print technology is linked with a more fundamental issue: the traditional Indian system for the transmission of knowledge. Hindus continued to regard oral communication as the most important mode of teaching, transmission of religious texts and secular knowledge as well as examination of students till the third century B.C. when written records became available. The Indian tradition attached the greatest importance to memory. The *Vedic* texts, called *Srutis* (literally meaning something that has been heard or revealed), had been passed on from one generation to another generation of *shishyas* (pupils) from the *guru* (teacher). The pupils were enjoined to memorise and recite them faithfully without altering them as many *Vedic* mantras (hymns) are used in different Hindu rituals. It is believed that if these are not recited with the proper accent they nullify all the virtues and merits that the sacrificer would acquire. Owing to the crucial role of memory in the preservation and transmission of knowledge, the major part of ancient Indian literature was written in the form of hymns, which were easy to reproduce owing to their rhyming quality[14]. Even after the development of *Sutra* style (concise writing) of prose around fifth century B.C., use of verse continued to be popular for writing *Vedic* literature: law books, epics and *Puranas.*

On the whole, use of print technology militated against the very heart of Indian systems for the transmission of knowledge. It attacked the essential assumptions and beliefs that made knowledge trustworthy, authoritative and valuable. Through the multiplication of texts, the printing machine threatened to snap the bond between the teacher and the disciple and weaken the priestly authority. The vested interest of the Brahmin priests and the *ulemas,* who also functioned as teachers, obstructed the knowledge revolution. By containing the spread of education to a limited section of people, these transmitters of knowledge made a negative impact on the linkages betweeen science and technology[15]. The practice of giving only informal knowledge about religious rituals to craftsmen and artisans had stunted their intellectual curiosity and receptivity to new ideas and technologies.

Sixthly, the *Bhakti* movement had also legitimised conservatism to some extent owing to its emphasis on devotion to Lord Krishna, *guru* or a holy book. Under its influence, the enterprising mercantile communities in Gujarat, Punjab and the other regions tended to become contemplative and inward-looking rather than innovative. The craftsmen and artisans, who acquired a new dignity as Bhaktas and saints, also imbibed the characteristic devotional fervour. Even this wave of egalitarianism could not bring the benefits of knowledge from the literate castes to the unlettered craftsmen. The persistent communication gap between the well-read and the illiterate was compounded by the absence of a vernacular prose-tradition which can be partly explained by the unfortunate non-acceptance of printing press technology. In the region of Punjab, where the literacy percentage was below ten per cent[16], the absence of a vernacular prose tradition was not surprising. In contrast, most of the books in England were printed in English from the very beginning. William Caxton, who brought the printing press from continental Europe to England, printed seventy-four titles in English out of a total of roughly ninety books.[17]

Lastly, the hierarchical structure of Indian society exercised a negative influence on the attitudes of the wealthier and better-educated Muslims and Sikhs who regarded craftsmen and artisans as their inferiors. Thus, social distance, which had undermined the self-confidence of the poor and unlettered men, was not conducive to a creative synthesis between intellectual theories and practical experience as well as to the generation of new ideas and labour-saving devices. Moreover, availability of abundant and cheap labour had rendered the capital intensive activity and extensive use of mechanical power unnecessary. This observation is broadly applicable to the development of scientific knowledge and technology including printing machines. In the case of Punjab, its open geographical frontier had obliged its inhabitants to focus their energies and resources on the cultivation of martial qualities and skills in order to cope with hordes of foreign invaders. In such a situation, intellectual pursuits were devalued and exchange of knowledge and skills between the conquerors and the vanquished people not possible. The craftsmen were, thus, obliged to rely on inherited skills and not acquisition of new skills. However, an acute awareness of threat to cultural, especially religious, identity under the colonial rule not only changed social equations but also valuation of Western science and technologies.

It is amply clear that the delay in the adoption of print technology in India can be explained by the convergence of a variety of factors/causes. The major communities Hindus, Sikhs and Muslims were compelled to shed their biases and reluctance when confronted with a different kind of challenge in the nineteenth century.

II

Socialisation of the Printing Press and its Diffusion in Colonial Punjab

What were the circumstances that obliged Indians to adopt printing technology? The social environment in which the

Indian people were introduced to various technological innovations could be described as one of religio-political domination. The factor of military conquest and political dominance assumed great significance in the transfer of technology and other communication innovations such as telegraph and railways in the last three decades of the 19th century when the British had established their hegemony. Before taking up discussion regarding the adoption of particular modes of print technology, it is relevant to present a brief view of the colonial milieu.

By the mid-nineteenth century, the political authority and trade monopoly of the East India Company had been curtailed. Queen Victoria's Proclamation (1858) had completed the process of transfer of power from the John Company to the British Parliament and the Crown. Two more important developments, which aided the consolidation of imperial hegemony over the Indian empire, were the removal of ban on missionary activities (1833) and Macaulay's Minute (1835). The use of military force could at best establish precarious control over the subject people. Hence, conquest of mind and colonisation of consciousness became a major imperial project, executed through an inter-linked and simultaneous process—demolition of Indian's pride and belief in their own systems of knowledge, religious and cultural values and projection of the superior Western culture, religion, sciences and arts.

Viewed in this context, transfer of novel artifacts or technologies to the colonies especially India was an integral part of the long-term British project of civilising mission and global hegemony[18]. Among the several groups, who introduced the print-technology, four agents were noteworthy: the merchants, the British officials, the Indians and the Christian missionaries —both European and American. The purpose, duration and nature of exposure of the colonial subjects to the imported technological innovations was determined by these agents' commitment to the ideals and visions of the British empire. Keeping in view the dominance of the imperial presence in the political, economic and even social process, the adoption of the printing press in India was essentially intrusive.

The intrusive process of adoption was three-staged[19] but it was not uniform throughout India as the military conquest of a particular territory, region or province and consolidation of administrative or political control over each one of them by the British was a long process spanning over a period of almost one century, i.e. 1757-1857. First, there was a period of introduction when the Bengalis, south Indians (Malayalis or Tamils), Marathas, Hindustanis and Punjabis attempted to use the printing press because they sought in general to learn and master the British ways. While these new methods may not have appeared to Indians as being completely superior to Asian ways, but were evidently a source of imperial power. Indian students in Western-styled schools and colleges, orphans and prisoners in orphanages and jails, employees and candidates for jobs in government offices and institutions used press or worked as printers, managers or technicians.

A second stage was the experiments in adaptation of Bengali or Punjabi culture to the printing press. At this stage, the Western educated urban elite tried to tailor the indigenous patterns to fit in with the British system. During the third stage, the Indians particularly Punjabis adopted the printing technology to meet their specific needs. Henceforth, the press was used as a tool on its own merits, i.e. as an effective medium of mass communication and not merely because the British rulers had used it. In the final stage, Indians in Bengal, western and south India and the United Provinces could use novel artifacts as tools not because these were fancy toys or as symbols of subservience or of their desire to become Westernised but because these were useful to protect their cultural identity and religious beliefs which had been denigrated and attacked by the colonial administrators-turned-ethnographers, sociologists and anthropologists of the Utilitarian school and aggressively undermined by the Christian missionaries.

It may be pointed out that Bengal and Punjab provide interesting cases for the students of reform process in Indian society as well as of the administrative and institutional mechanisms evolved for the articulation of colonialism and its ideology from the 1750s to the 1940s. The former exemplified enthusiastic but somewhat uncritical and ambivalent response to the introduction and dissemination of Western education, ideologies, technologies, scientific and cultural artifacts. The latter represented the apotheosis of the process of the colonisation of consciousness and maturity of the hegemonic ideology. Both these provinces of British-India represent two models of the articulation of Hindu consciousness—universalistic and exclusionist through the intensive use of print-technology. However, I shall draw my illustrations from the Punjab as its people became the most enthusiastic participants in the Arya Samaj experiment of ideological propaganda through the coupling of the traditional oral mode with the modern print technology.

Turning to the issue of the diffusion of print technology, I don't propose to discuss the entire range of its innovations. It is relevant, however, to focus briefly on the role of the American Presbyterian missionaries in providing training in technological apparatus, appropriate social organisation, linguistic and institutional models to the social reform leaders of Hindus, Muslims and Sikhs in the Punjab. It had unintended implication for changes in their conceptualisation of religion and its linkage with worldly goals including economic and political. As founders of the Ludhiana Mission in the 1830s, William Jones and John Newton played a major role in introducing the entire package of printing technology[20]. Instead of importing skilled technicians from Europe, John Newton, who was incharge of the Mission Press, had trained the young inmates of Christian orphanages and the boys from untouchable and other lower castes, with the help of one Bengali Christian compositor. These Indian apprentices, who honed their skills while printing Christian propaganda literature in Persian, Urdu, Punjabi, Kashmiri, Sindhi, Chamba, Pahari, Tibetan and English, gradually learnt to operate founts without direct missionary supervision. For example, one promising apprentice later on rose to be the grey-haired General Manager of the Ludhiana Mission Press which has coordinated the publication programme of the American Bible and Tract Society, the Punjab Bible and Religious Books Society, the Presbyterian Board of

Foreign Missions, the Christian Vernacular Education Society and the Hyderabad Mission.

Another major as well as exemplary missionary achievement was the creation of a pool of expert personnel for writing lucid tracts and pamphlets for its propaganda. Even more crucial to the project of Indianisation of Christianity was the enlistment of Punjabi scholars, writers, school teachers, clerks and book-retailers who provided support system for the printing press. For example, Imam-ud-din not only received baptism himself in 1866 but also converted his friends namely, Maulana Safdar Ali. Written in simple, natural, polished, terse yet attractive style, his tracts and pamphlets served as models of apologetic literature both for the Punjabi Christians and Indian social reformers whether liberal or reactionary.

The Mission presses took a major step forward towards professionalisation of religious propaganda. It is best exemplified in the compilation of bibliographies of Christian literature such as Weitbretch's *Descriptive Catalogue* and his bibliographic articles in the missionary magazine entitled *The Indian Evangelical Review.* An integral part of their drive was the coordination of the various publication units of north India who sent representatives to conferences, compiled catalogues of their works, tried to avoid duplication of effort and to discover weak areas in their common lists.

Equally significant was the missionary initiative in creating a base for the standardisation of Indian vernacular languages particularly Punjabi and Urdu for its long-term goal of spreading Christianity throughout the Punjab as in the rest of India. By publishing *Punjabi New Testament,* the first translation of any Western book in type-print of Gurmukhi script, William Carey had provided a sound basis for modern Punjabi prose-writing, spelling, word-formation and stabilization of the ever-changing Gurmukhi script. While Munshi Kanshi Ram Khatri wrote the first *Punjabi Grammar* (1810). John Newton's *Idiomatic Sentences in English and Punjabi* (1846), *A Grammar of Punjabi Language* (1851), and *Punjabi Language Dictionary* (1854) were the first such works to be produced and printed in the Punjab.[21] It may be mentioned that the Christian missionary's lobbying for script reform and their ground work in linguistics had facilitated the task of standardising the Devnagari script by Swami Dayanand and his lieutenants in the Punjab and the second generation leaders of the Arya Samaj movement.

By the 1880s, socio-religious reformers became acutely aware of the powerful role of print-technology in the persistent and aggressive missionary offensive on the religious beliefs, knowledge systems and social institutions of all the three communities, particularly of the Hindus—the largest community in India. Their perception of the long-term involvement of missionaries in the imperial project of cultural hegemonization and multiple subjugation of the Indian people was based on the content of mission literature and official publications. For example, Robert Clark, one of the Presbyterian missionaries in the Punjab, painted a miserable picture of the intellectual calibre of the Punjabis[22].

> The Punjabis, who do not know English remain babies all their lives. They have no love for literature, for they have no literature to love in Urdu. Their minds are never enriched with any stores from better minds, and the consequence is that native Christians have little influence or no influence on the educated classes.

The issue that disturbed Joseph Warren of Allahabad Mission and other ethnocentric Westerners including colonial administrators-turned-ethnographers, sociologists and anthropologists was the confident ethnocentrism of the Punjabis. That the 'Eastern' people could be ignorant of Truth (as Westerners conceived it) was understandable, but they could fail to perceive the superiority of Western truths was amazing to Warren. He inter-linked cultural backwardness of Hindus with their scientific backwardness and arrogantly observed "We have to teach people not only religion but also history and science[23]". Such negative commentary obliged Hindus, Muslims and Sikhs to modernize their religious traditions and social institutions but they were not willing to adopt Western culture in toto. For their cultural survival, they chose the alternative of selective modernisation of their tradition.

III

Swami Dayanand's Response to Western Science and Technology

Having watched and learnt the technical and administrative skills of the printing press and the process of its manipulation by the Christian missions and the British rulers in establishing their cultural hegemony during the past few decades, the educated Hindus were eager to experiment with the printed word for articulating their hopes and fears, predicament and problems of adjustment in a new colonial milieu. Despite the increased job opportunities, created by the new educational policy, new administrative and legal system, new technologies and new patterns of trade (both national and international), the urban Hindus (representing the emergent middle class), realised that the colonial rule was not an unmixed blessing. The humiliation implicit in the assumed superiority of the white 'bureaucrats' in their daily dealings with the Indians was hard to digest. The well-placed Hindus, therefore, needed an ideology, a psychological anchor, which could bolster their nebulous identity and dignity. They also required a programme of action which could make their daily social interaction meaningful and conducive to their communitarian cohesiveness without impeding their chances of individually competing successfully in the new set-up.[24]

The Punjabi Hindu and Sikh intellectuals, after initial acceptance of the Brahmo Samaj (established in 1863), found it difficult to identify with its socially radical, syncretistic, rational and theistic ideology as an alternative. They discovered their new faith and identity through Swami Dayanand, who expounded the Arya Samaj ideology in the course of his lectures at Lahore in 1877. By giving an integrated view of India's past, present and future, the wandering ascetic had provided intellectual reassurance and pride to the first generation of middle class Hindus and imparted dignity to their identity, being constantly undermined by the colonial regime and the Christian missionaries. Through Arya ideology and programme, which encompassed doctrinal issues, socio-religious reform, uplift of women, regeneration of a Hindu nation by education, popularisation of Hindi, *shuddhi* and *swadeshi,* he had offered a wide choice of areas of action to each person according to his inclination and class interest.

Swami Dayanand developed his communication strategy for the dissemination of his ideology stage-by-stage[25]. His prolonged interaction with the anglicised Indians, particularly, Brahmos in Calcutta played an important role in the transformation of his ideology and reform strategies. In the first phase 1868 to 1871, he used traditional forms of public debate or *shashtrath* and education. Swami Dayanand's experiment of using Sanskrit for communication for his version of Hinduism with a view to reorienting the Brahminical concepts and practices also yielded no positive result. It may be pointed out that the Calcutta experience had transformed him from an ascetic into an action-oriented socio-religious reformer who discarded Sanskrit in favour of Hindi and privileged printed work over traditional modes.

In the second phase 1872 to 1875, he continually experimented with various forms of organisation and proselytisation. In Mathura, he founded an *Arya Sabha* and a journal, *Arya Prakash,* but neither succeeded. At this point of time, he had neither sufficient funds nor disciples. It was his meeting with Sir Syed Ahmed Khan which led to the writing of *Satyarth Prakash,* a comprehensive statement of his ideas and beliefs. First published in 1875, revised and reprinted in 1884, this book was to become a major influence on the thinking of Hindus in the Punjab and north-western India. Despite his initial success in Maharashtra and Gujarat, his ideas attracted very few people as disciples.

In the third and final phase, from 1875 onwards, Swami Dayanand fully concentrated on propaganda through the press and platform. By establishing an apex body called *Propkarini Sabha* on August 16, 1880 at Meerut, he had ensured the protection of his intellectual property rights. Apart from his influential book *Satyarth Prakash*, he had written lucid commentaries on the *Vedas, Upanishads* and on other important religious books, as well as conduct-books as *Sanskar Vidhi* and numerous tracts in order to mould the thinking, attitudes and behaviour patterns of men and women for knitting them into a religious community. It was through the use of print technology that Swami Dayanand's message reached the educated people who carried it to the other literate and the illiterate men and women through lectures and readings which was an important programme of Arya Samaj *mandirs.* It needs to be pointed out that the spread of education through Anglo-vernacular institutions in west Punjab—especially in the Lahore-Jalandhar belt and *gurukuls* for boys and girls in the rural areas of south-east Punjab, occupied a central place in the Arya Samaj programme.

Swami ji's growing faith in the immense power of the printed word led him to supervise the entire production process—from proof-reading to binding of books, tracts and magazines. With the geographical and programmatic expansion of the Arya Samaj movement, demand for printed material increased so much that it was no longer economical to get his writings, especially *Satyarth Prakash* and *Sanskar Vidhi* and important tracts published at the Lazanes and Nirnaya Sagar Press, Varanasi. Hence in 1880, he started another press known as Arya Prakash Mantralaya, later known as Vedic Mantralaya in Kashi.

For an understanding of the Arya rationale underlying acceptance of Western science and its allied technologies for the reformation of Hinduism, it may be pointed out that it rested on functionalism. The entire thrust of Dayanand's response was neither to contest nor to refute it. A new mythology of the Hindu past was invoked in order to legitimise adaptation of Western scientific knowledge and the new technology of printing. No longer regarded as the monopoly of the 'white' imperialists, science was incorporated into the Hindu traditions which had been rediscovered and contextualised with the contemporary world and its problems. However, Swami Dayanand's disciples, e.g. Pandit Guru Dutt Vidyarthi, Lala Hans Raj, Lala Lajpat Rai and others, despite being partial products of Western scholarship, found it hard to digest deft but biased missionary use of works of Monier Williams, Max Mueller and Indian

Sanskritologists for ridiculing Arya claims about the advanced *Vedic* civilisation.

Amongst them, Pandit Guru Dutt[26] was the most well-equipped to challenge the arrogant European representations of India's past. As a Professor of Science, he was not only familiar with the European intellectual currents but was also in daily contact with the upholders of these ideologies. Besides, his growing emotional commitment to *Vedic* truth and *Sanskritic* studies gave him a special advantage over the other educated Punjabis. He recognised the urgency of rejecting the substandard and biased European scholarship on the *Vedas* which found general and uncritical acceptance among the English-educated Punjabis, having no knowledge of Sanskrit scriptures. Through a combined use of Dayanand's method of interpreting the *Vedas* and his own scientific training, Pandit Guru Dutt exposed the ignorance of European scholars and the 'derivative position'[27] of Western civilisation, especially science and technology. His writings and lectures restored the faith of the Aryas and the other Hindus in Dayanand's vision of India's past, infallibility of the *Vedas* and superiority of Sanskrit and projected them as pathways to future greatness. Despite his scientific background, he became gradually intolerant of any criticism of his mentor's views and of moderate conceptualisation of the goals and strategies of the Arya Samaj movement[28]. It is not relevant to discuss here the long-term implications of his rigid views for the ideological development and reform programmes of the Aryas who were to bifurcate themselves into two wings—moderate and militant.

For the Arya leadership whether moderate or militant, it was tactical to maintain continual interaction between ideology and action as well as to gear their communication apparatus to the changing demands of the colonial milieu of intense religious competition and missionary assault upon Hindus, Muslims and Sikhs. The printing technology was to be used as the major instrument for a three-fold purpose: (i) for inspiring faith and commitment among young boys and girls and women to *Arya* ideals and Dayanand's vision of past, present and future; (ii) for an effective implementation of its programme of socio-religious reform, especially women's uplift; (iii) for fixing the identity and position of the Arya Samaj within the Hindu universe and in relation to other religious communities.

In order to achieve the broad objective of creating a new unified Hindu community, the Lahore Arya Samaj split its bid into two parts: (i) crystallisation of the ten principles of the Arya Samaj and framing of its by-laws by a committee of three members, namely Lala Sain Das, Lala Jivan Das and Lala Mul Raj on July 24, 1877;[29] (ii) printing its multiple copies for wide circulation. The first generation of Arya leadership proposed to capture the hearts and minds of the literate castes among Hindus, who felt most the pain of alienation from the traditional Punjabi society and adjustment with new forms of employment, communication and cultural milieu of colonial institutions. An urgent need for dignity and identity propelled these fast-growing marginal men to accept new concepts and make new commitments. Their literacy skills made them ideal converts and communicators of Arya ideology whose services could be used for expanding the network of Arya *biradari* in the urban and rural areas of north India, particularly central and south-east Punjab now called Haryana.

The first experiments with the print media were made by the individual Aryas, who published tracts and pamphlets on specific issues to provide explanation of general Samaj ideology[30]. But an effective communication with the potential audience came only with the establishment of institutional periodicals and dailies. Among the first Samaj periodicals was the *Arya*, started and edited by Lala Rattan Chand Barry (Lahore) in1882. In view of the numerous misunderstandings regarding the goals of the Arya Samaj, the editor hoped that his newspaper would, if possible, "blunt the shaft of our detractors". According to an advertisement in *The Tribune* dated June 13, 1882, this journal was devoted to "Aryan philosophy, art and science, literature and religion, embracing the views and opinions of its readers on these topics."[31] Obviously, printing technology had enabled the literate Punjabis to engage in a continuous dialogue with the editors and the other readers, belonging to the gradually emerging new socio-cultural groups among the Hindus of north India.

Publication of the second periodical entitled the *Regenerator of Aryavarta* in 1882 (an English weekly) had been inspired by the suggestion of Lala Salig Ram, the proprietor of the Arya Press.[32] Jointly edited by Lala Hans Raj (1860-1938) and Pandit Guru Dutt (1864-1890), this weekly remained the voice of the Lahore Samaj during its life span of barely two years. It may be mentioned that Lahore remained the major centre of Samaj publications, the source of news and the debating forum of ideological issues through the entire course of the Arya Samaj movement. Other towns like Ludhiana, Jalandhar, Multan and Ferozepur produced their own publications in response to the growing vigour and membership of their units but Lahore dominated.

It must be pointed out the new literate elites (65 per cent among them being Hindus especially the three commercial castes *Khatris, Banias* and *Aroras*)[33] increasingly used the printed word for reforming the Hindu tradition. Their growing awareness of the crucial link between scientific knowledge including technological expertise and socio-cultural change led the English-educated Punjabis to invest in the development of infrastructure. It included moveable typesets, founts for vernacular languages, equipment for lithography and iron-printing machines for the publication of newspapers, periodicals, posters, pamphlets and tracts with suitable illustrations. Thus, there was a dramatic increase in the number of newspapers and periodicals during the years between 1880 and 1904 as the following table shows:[34]

Table I: Number of Newspapers in Punjabi Five Year Averages 1880-1904

Year	*Average Number of Newspapers*
1880-1884	39.20
1885-1889	66.20
1890-1894	66.00
1895-1899	54.60
1900-1904	141.80

Their number waxed and waned under the pressure of various factors, not required to be discussed here. However, it acted as a reliable indicator of the expansion of literacy among different religious communities as the following table illustrates:[35]

Table II: Literacy by Religion for Punjab and Delhi 1891-1921

Year	*Hindu*	*Muslim*	*Sikh*	*Christian*
1891	530,875	161,365	85,007	29,661
1901	602,148	207,188	118,445	34,538
1911	-	-	-	-
1921	544,647	201,504	160,860	39,789

It is evident that the Hindus formed the majority of the emerging educated elite who also led in their knowledge of English. Their long tradition of literacy and cultural adjustment had enabled them not only to survive but also to prosper in some instances under the Mughal and Sikh rule. However, their cultural creativity, apart from social defence mechanism, had been activated by their realisation that the British rule had posed a fundamental challenge to the existing order and its underlying assumptions. This expanding awareness of change is reflected in the Arya institutional innovations as well as in their use of new modes of communication especially print-technology. In the next section, I have discussed the Arya publicists' effective use of press for recasting Hindu consciousness and strengthening their group solidarity.

IV

Recasting Hindu Consciousness Through Print

The crucial role of print-technology in recasting Hindu consciousness became visible in the Arya mobilisation of public opinion regarding the radical reform of life-cycle rituals which would separate their social universe from that of the Sanatanists. It was one of the key concerns for the Arya reformers because only a few Hindus had followed Swami Dayanand's instructions regarding the proper performance of birth, marriage and death rituals contained in *Sanskar Vidhi.* For illustrating my point, I have chosen to focus on their press campaign for two issues requiring wide acceptance: new death rituals and comprehensive marriage reform.

The first issue was the wide acceptance of new death rituals. It was believed that a wide publicity to the exemplary conduct of individual Aryas through newspapers, periodicals and pamphlets would have a lasting impact on the public mind. Obviously, the process of constructing separate ritual boundaries between the Aryas and the orthodox Sanatanists needed to be pushed to a decisive point through publication of the exemplary conduct of individual Aryas in newspapers, pamphlets and periodicals. By extolling the courageous and manly conduct of Pandit Guru Dutt (one of the first to practise his belief in the new *rites de passage* on the death of his parents despite threats of social boycott from the members of his castes), the *Arya Patrika,* dated November 15, 1887 had underlined the definition and implications of being a real Arya. Similar reports of Arya death ceremonies in its issues of January 4 and November 8, 1887 and March 20, 1888 and also in the issues of *The Tribune,* September 4 and 11, 1889 had reached thousands of people owing to the facility of printing more than a thousand copies which exchanged hands among numerous readers. Those, who sought to reject the traditional rituals, were boosted by the rationalisation of new practices in such Arya tracts as Durga Prasad's *Shraaddha* (A Feast and Charity in the Memory of Ancestors, 1892) and Swatma Nand's *Mritak Shraaddha Khandan* (Refutation of Shraaddha Ceremony, 1895).[36]

Easy availability of printed material and its wider circulation had facilitated the movement of news, ideas and the demonstration effect of a radical social action beyond narrow territorial boundaries. In the present context, practice of new life-cycle ceremonies gradually ceased either to shock the orthodox Hindus or provoke their hostility. Obviously, changes in the self-image and world-view of the Aryas had received social legitimacy by the turn of the century. Separated from the surrounding Hindu society, the Aryas forged bonds of brotherhood with those who shared not merely reformed religious beliefs but also a socio-cultural universe through the print media.

The second issue chosen for public debate was the adoption of marriage rituals prescribed in the *Sanskar Vidhi,* which symbolised a frontal assault on the traditional Hindu socio-cultural organisation. The question of marriage reform was given prominent coverage in the Arya print media because it touched two sensitive areas: first, "the role of women in Hindu society and second, the qualitative break from the existing social groups"[37]. In fact, the reformation of marriage ceremonies which was crucial to the relations between the Arya and the other Hindus, implicated an intensive social introspection and rethinking on the related issues of child-marriage and widow-remarriage from the angle of national regeneration.

The relevant question to be raised is: How far was the Arya leadership successful in using the print media for sharpening their group consciousness of their unique cultural identity and heritage through a multi-pronged campaign for the reform of marriage rituals? Between the period from 1880 to 1886, the Aryas remained busy in popularising simplified marriage ceremonies as prescribed in *Sanskar Vidhi* and discarding more elaborate and expensive ones in practice. While their tracts, journals and speeches focused on explaining the significance and meaning of reformed practices, the Arya dailies filled their columns with reports of Samaj marriages. Reports of such marriages in the issues of *Arya Patrika* from March to August 1888, had consciously moulded public opinion in two directions: as a model for the enterprising members and as an encouragement to those who feared social disapproval. For example, its correspondent while describing the marriage of the daughter of a prominent Arya Lala Amir Chand in its issue dated March 27, 1888, applauded his "determined character and true Arya views". He also underlined the positive impact of the actual marriage ceremony in removing misunderstandings about Arya customs and institutions. His conclusive observations underlined the *elan vital* of the Arya Samaj movement: "...and it is deeds which will win us the sympathy and cooperation of the people and not empty lectures".

The Aryas had used the printed word in an innovative way while resolving the problem of finding suitable matches within their expanding community. Separated from their natal families either by distance or ideology, they developed a new marriage institution—the newspaper advertisements. Beginning in 1883, the Samaj dailies advertised requests for an "Arya gentleman who should be sound in health, good character and gives the pledge to never enter into bigamy or polygamy"[38] and for a bride "who decides to get married in strict accordance with the *Vedic* rites"[39]. By 1884, the matrimonial notice was a standard item in many Samaj publications. In addition to the traditional criteria of noble family or lineage, wealth and colour, these notices stressed new qualifications: English education of the potential groom or a family dedicated to Samaj ideals. Proficiency in the anglicised world did not replace the traditional criteria of status, but added familial dimensions to that status.[40]

The Arya experience of using print technology in recasting self-view, world-view and material-cum-spiritual goals of the 'enlightened and educated Hindus' helped the leadership to gain support for the more sensitive issue of widow-remarriage among non-Arya Hindus. They faced a difficult question: How to locate widows willing to remarry? The appearance of new publications, namely the *Social Reformer* and *Marriage Advertiser,* offered a practical solution. A new column in the *Regenerator of Aryavrata,* dated February 11, 1884, represented the enthusiastic welcome to the new journal by the Arya activists. Expressing sympathy with its aims and objects, it gave publicity to the cause of widow-remarriages by focusing public attention on the cause of widow-remarriages by focusing public attention on the full page advertisements of names of widows, willing to remarry. The quality of relationship between technology and religion varied according to the skill of the Arya publicists engaged in conducting campaigns on specific issues. For example, the Amritsar Samaj's sustained publicity given to the marriage of one Arora couple on September 10, 1885 and of a Brahmin widow on August 22, 1886 through newspaper notices, reports and meetings turned them into grand public events. It was indicative of an attitudinal change among the high castes.

According to the reports in the *Arya Patrika* dated September 12, 1885, these unconventional social events caused immense excitement among women who used to assemble in large numbers on the balconies to witness the marriage ceremonies in the adjacent *samaj mandir* (temple). Encouraged by growing public interest and approval (though not entirely devoid of controversy), the Lahore Arya Samaj and its branch at Kohat extended their full support to the activists at Amritsar in strengthening the widow remarriage campaign.[41]

It may be pointed out that the social reform leadership increasingly utilised print technology for reaching the educated Punjabis upon whom it depended as potential allies and as carriers of day-to-day news about its activities to the illiterate. As a result of positive and extensive press-coverage, new life-cycle ceremonies and Samaj-sponsored marriages for virgin-widows gained greater public approval and legitimacy. Their impact was reinforced by the publication of Arya pamphlets. Usually dramatic in its presentation, this genre of literature presented Samaj ideology in numerous forms—lectures, dialogues, moral tales, etc. Among the tracts on the question of widow-remarriage and child marriage are included *Do Hindu Bewa Aurton Ki Batcheet* (A Dialogue Between Two Hindu Widows), *Risala-i-dharam Mitra* (The Friend of Religion) and *Brahamacharya versus Child-Marriage.*[42] Despite publication of actual widow-remarriages and persuasive Arya tracts, the new social practice did not gain wide currency in the remaining part of the nineteenth century. However, an effective use of print technology had enabled the Arya Samaj to dilute vehement orthodox opposition and made the social climate congenial for those who contemplated such a step.

V

Conclusion

The foregoing discussion has made it amply clear that print technology had enabled the Arya leadership and publicists to bring about distinct changes in the self-image and world-view of their co-religionists. Firstly, it facilitated the creation and development of a protestant or scriptural identity based on the

Vedas. During the two crucial decades from the 1880s to 1900, a number of factors, particularly a sense of fierce pride in the reinterpreted past with its heritage and a purified reformed future, commitment to religious ideology and long-term communitarian and political goals, a shared memory of bitter struggles against Christian missionaries and intense religious competition with Muslims and Sikhs, had contributed to the creation of a new unified Arya community. Through the publication of numerous editions and extensive distribution of printed copies of *Sanskar Vidhi,* the daily lives of a sizeable number of the urban-educated as well as semi-literate Aryas were disciplined. It also helped in giving social legitimacy to ritual innovations which were gradually adopted by the Arya families.

It is significant that the printed word did not replace the traditional modes of communication and mobilisation. A judicious combination of congregational and itinerant propaganda through singing groups *(Bhajan mandalis)* and the printed word (e.g. Swami Dayanand's books, particularly, *Satyarth Prakash, Sanskar Vidhi,* Arya leaders' biographies, newspapers, periodicals and tracts in Urdu, Hindi and English) as well as the exemplary conduct of Arya leaders had facilitated internalisation and articulation of three identities—Arya, Hindu and Indian. The *Punjabee* (founded and edited by Lala Lajpat Rai from 1904-1911) and earlier Arya Samaj periodicals conveyed these complexities to the readers, moulded their choices, loyalties and simultaneous assertion of one identity or the other suiting their interests.

Secondly, the printing press became the major instrument not only for the transfer of Western knowledge and its concepts, e.g. enlightenment, rationality and scientism but also for their appropriation by the Arya reformers for a two-fold purpose. In the first instance, these were used as a yardstick while reinterpreting the central tenets of the ancient scriptures of the Hindus in order to project their religion as progressive and scientific. Pandit Guru Dutt went to great lengths to establish the scientific nature of the *Vedas*, by using the scheme of reinterpretation laid down by Swami Dayanand. Going to the logical extreme, he maintained that the ancient Aryans had known about and invented all the gadgetry of the contemporary world.[43]

It may be pointed out that Guru Dutt's preoccupation with science and technology was not a matter of individual interest. These branches of knowledge had begun to attract the attention of the young educated Punjabis in the 1880s. As students of Government College, Lahore, Pandit Guru Dutt, Ruchi Ram Sahni and other intelligent citizens had spent their leisure time in discussing and examining the implications and relevance of European social theories and scientific knowledge for shaping modern India. While the former's interest in Western science was influenced by his religiosity, the latter's crusade for its popularisation was guided by development ethics. Acutely conscious of social discrimination in daily life, both of them had shared patriotic impluses when they chose to study Western science and adopt selective technologies such as the printing press. While the Arya Samaj Institute (established in 1884) represented an effort to find a new equation between science and religion, Ruch Ram Sahni's Punjab Science Institute (founded in 1885) symbolised the brave struggle of intellectuals to pursue science in a colonial society.[44]

REFERENCES

1. Francis Bacon, *Advancement of Learning: New Atlantis* (New York: The Colonial Press, 1899), 366: Aphorism 129.
2. Marshall McLuhan, *The Gutenberg Galaxy: The Making of Typographic Man*, London, Routledge & Kegan Paul, 1962; George Steiner, *Language and Silence*, London, Faber & Faber, 1967; for insights into the subtler effects of print on human consciousness, see Walter J. Ong, *The Presence of the Word: Some Prolegomena for Cultural and Religious History*, New Haven & London, Yale University Press, 1967.
3. Edward C. Sachau (trans.), *Alberuni's India* (London: Paul, 1910), 170-171.
4. Anonymous, *Tarikh-i-Kashmir*. Cited in A. Rahman, 'Paper Technology in India', in A. Rahman (ed.), *History of Indian Science, Technology and Culture* (Delhi: Oxford University Press, 1999), 264.

5. Sujan Rai, *Khulasat-i-Tawarikh*. Cited in ibid., 265.
6. D.C. Sircar, *Indian Epigraphy* (Delhi: Motilal Banarsidass, 1965), 67.
7. A.K. Priolkar, *The Printing Press in India* (Bombay: Marathi Samaj Dhana Mandal, 1958), 7-8, 38.
8, Francis Goldie, *First Christian Missions to the Great Mogul* (London, 1897), 63; for a detailed list of books presented to Akbar, see E. MacLagan, *The Jesuits and the Great Mogul* (London, 1932), 191.
9. Joseph Needham, *Science and Civilization in China*, Vol. I (Cambridge: Cambridge University Press, 1985), 361-362.
10. Irfan Habib, "Changes in Technology of Medieval India", in *Studies in History*, 2, no. 11 (1980), 38-39.
11. Francis Robinson, "Technology and Religious Change: Islam and the Impact of Print", in *Modern Asian Studies*, 27, No. 1 (1993), 237.
12. Ibid., 238-239.
13. A. Rahman, cit., n. 4, 262; Thomas Carter, "Islam a Barrier to Printing", in *The Moslem World*, 33 (1943), 213-216.
14. My information in the forgoing paragraph is based on R.S. Sharma, "Indian Civilization", in Harold D. Lasswell, Daniel Lerner and Hans Spier (eds), *Propaganda and Communication in World History*, 3 vols (Honolulu: The University Press of Hawaii, 1979), 177.
15. A. Rahman, cit. n. 4,262.
16. *Census of India* 1931 (Delhi Government of India, 1932), Vol. 17, Pt I, 267.
17. Elizabeth L. Eisenstein, *The Printing Press as an Agent of Change: Communication and Cultural Transformation in Early Modern Europe*, Cambridge, Cambridge University Press, 1979.
18. For an insightful discussion of the 'Civilization mission' of the imperial powers, particularly Britain and its linkage with the Western project of global hegemony, see Michael A. Das, *Machines as the Measure of Man: Science, Technologies and Ideologies of Western Domination* (Delhi: Oxford University Press, 1989), 129-199.
19. Emmett Davis, *Press and Politics in British Western Punjab 1836-1947* (New Delhi: Academic Publications, 1983), 8-9.
20. Ibid., 132, 213, 216.
21. For information regarding the work of the Allahabad Mission Press and Ludhiana Mission Press and their publications, see Emmett Davis, op. cit., 43-72.
22. Robert Clark, *A Brief Account of Thirty Years of Missionary Society in the Punjab and Sindh* (Lahore: Albert Press, 1883),43.
23. Joseph Warren, *A Glance Backward at Fifteen Years of Missionary Life in North India* (Philadelphia: Presbyterian Board of Publications, 1856), 222-223.

24. For an interesting analysis of the predicament of the emergent Hindu middle classes and their response to the Arya ideology and programme, see Kenneth W. Jones, *Arya Dharm: Hindu Consciousness in 19th Century Punjab* (Delhi: Manohar Book Service, 1976), 18-29, 58-66.
25. For a detailed discussion of Swami Dayanand's experiments between 1868–1875, see Satyaketu Vidyalankar and Professor Hardutt, *Arya Samaj Ka Itihas,* in Hindi (Delhi: Arya Swadhyaya Kendra, 1982), 337–345.
26. I have drawn my information about his ideology from Lajpat Rai, *Life of Pandit Guru Dutt Vidyarthi,* M.A. (Lahore: Virjanand Press, 1981), 36; Lala Jivan Das (ed.), *The Works of Pandit Guru Dutt Vidyarthi,* Lahore, The Punjab Printing Works, 1902.
27. Kenneth W. Jones, op. cit., n. 24, 166.
28. Lala Jivan Das (ed.), op. cit., 281-282.
29. Kenneth W. Jones, op. cit., n. 24,37.
30. Among the first such tract writers was Bawa Narain Singh who published his first tract in Punjabi (1878) and the second one in Urdu (1882) from Chashma-i-Nur Press (Amritsar) and Arya Press (Lahore) respectively.
31. Quoted from an advertisement in *The Tribune*, June 13, 1882, 11.
32. Kenneth W. Jones, op. cit., n. 24, 46-47.
33. Census of Punjab, Report 1911, 322. For a statistical picture, see the following table:

Literacy of Major Castes—Number of Literates per 'le'

Hindu		*Muslims*	
Khatri	250	Sayyid	83
Aggarwal	212	Qureshi	77
Arora	210	Sheikh	74
Brahaman	113	Khoja	58
		Pathan	53

For literacy of major castes in English, see *Census of Punjab, Report 1891*, lxix, 253 and Appendix C, Abstract 61:

Literacy in English by Caste in Punjab

Caste	*No. of Literates*	*No. of Literates in English*
Khatri	99,405	42,21
Brahmans	116,542	2,697
Sheikhs (Muslims)	23,181	13,38
Aroras	138,928	1,313
Banias	103,928	1153

Total no. of Punjabis literate in English: 19,274.

34. N. Gerald Barrier and Paul Wallace, *The Punjab Press* (East Lansing, Michigan: The Research Committee on the Punjab and the Asian Studies Centre, Michigan State University, 1970), 165.
35. *Census of Punjab, Report 1901*, 263-264.
36. Durga Prasad, *The Shraaddha,* (Lahore, Virjanand Press, 1892), and Swatma Nand, *Mritak Shraaddha Khandan,* (Lahore: Virjanand Press), 1895.
37. Kenneth W. Jones, op. cit., n. 24, 98.
38. *Arya,* February 1883,262.
39. *Arya Patrika,* May 4, 1888, 8.
40. For example see *Regenerator for Aryavarta,* August 11, 1884.
41. For details see *Arya Patrika*, August 24, 1886. 8; *The Tribune,* August 28, 1886, 7; *Arya Patrika,* August 31, 1886, September 7 and 8, 1886, 5.
42. For details see Lala Jivan Das, *Do Hindu Bewa Aurton Ki Batcheet,* transl. by H.L. Saxena, (Lahore, Arya Pustkalya, 1891); Munshi Chatar Bihari Lal, *Risala-i-dhaam Mitra,* Sadhaura: Bilain Press, 1893; Atma Ram, *Masala-i-Niyog* (Principles of Widow Marriage), Lahore, Mufid- i-' Am Press, 1888.
43. Lala Jivan Das (ed.), *The Works of Pandit Guru Dutt Vidyarthi*, cit., 215-216.
44. For a critical analysis of Ruchi Ram Sahni's views on Western science and technology and his contribution to its popularisation, see Kamlesh Mohan, "Ruchi Ram Sahni: Pursuit of Science in the Colonial Society", in N.K. Sehgal and Satpal Sangwan and Subodh Mohanty (eds), *Uncharted Terrain: Essays on Science Popularization in Pre-Independence India* (Delhi: Vigyan Prasar, 2000), 107-124.

4

Ruchi Ram Sahni and the Pursuit of Science in a Colonial Society

Ruchi Ram Sahni represents that generation of Punjabis which laid not only the foundations of the middle classes in this region but also actively participated in the socio-cultural and intellectual fermentation, resulting from the East-West encounter. Interestingly, the small number of urban mercantile families, who were exposed to the initial blast of Western ideas and cultural innovations following the annexation of Punjab in March 1849 had also been obliged to reckon with the peasant ethos, oral tradition and popular culture brought by the sons (rarely daughters) of the ambitious village literate and rich peasants to the towns and cities of Lahore, Amritsar, Rawalpindi and Multan where they came for education and later employment.[1]

Apart from experiencing the tensions and contradictions in this peculiar socio-cultural milieu, Ruchi Ram as an Indian had also to carry the grievous burden of colonial domination. Creativity and leadership roles of this generation in intellectual, social, political and cultural fields depended firstly on their perception and awareness of their altered circumstances, produced by the colonial states' transformatory programme and policies under the banner of development and modernisation. Secondly, these depended on the extent of their dissatisfaction with the traditional patterns of culture and intensity of resentment and apprehension aroused by the colonial hegemonisation through cultural and intellectual engineering.

These two points are equally relevant in any discussion on the cultivation of literature, arts and science under a foreign rule. Recent studies on the place of science in colonial projects have shown beyond doubt that science was inextricably woven into the whole fabric of colonialism. Both were locked into each other, sometimes in an inverse relationship. The state claimed superiority in terms of physical power, resources and race. Science, which claimed superiority in terms of knowledge, was ultimately co-opted by the colonial state and helped it to dismiss other epistemologies as primitive. Several colonial scientists felt uncomfortable yet they had to perform a dual role—to serve the colonial state and to pursue their intellectual calling, i.e. the cultivation of science.

As social control was regarded as the pre-condition for the perpetuation of the politico-economic control and authority of the raj, the colonial sociologist, anthropologist and ethnographer joined hands to produce scholarly tomes and empirical studies about Punjab—its ecological conditions, cadastral resources, its multi-religious society, institutions, manners, customs as well as religious and cultural traditions.[2] Under such compelling demands the national-minded scientists had achieved distinction in their profession and partial success in popularising science mainly on account of their personal commitment, and creative energy rather than through state patronage. In order to appreciate the magnitude of their enterprise in a predominantly rural society of Punjab, we need to understand not only the common cultural framework of this region but also the role of the new catalytic agents, introduced by the British.

I

Socio-cultural Milieu of Punjab

Ruchi Ram Sahni grew amidst a whirlpool of changes triggered by the installation of a new ruling elite, and the import of an equally new layer of experts, Indian but non-Punjabi. However, my intention in describing the socio-cultural universe of this region is to underline the shared aims of the movements for popularising science and for reforming religious beliefs, social practices and attitudes of the people, i.e. to create a progressive society.[3] While the scientist used the discourse of rationality for enhancing the common man's understanding about the working of natural phenomena and facilitate their productive control, the socio-religious activist and reformer made it an instrument for combatting polytheism, superstitious beliefs which had blocked the growth of individuality and reconstitution of contemporary society. In order to achieve their goal, both were required to understand the working of their societies in which they lived.

The socio-cultural universe which Ruchi Ram Sahni tried to challenge needs to be understood from the perspective of a total field of religion[4] as a common framework holding together its entire structure. The clientele of priestly religion despite its dependence on scriptures, often traversed the territory of popular religion, bowed to its presiding deities and sought their intercession in human affairs. In contrast the believers in saint cults, nature-gods, spirits and demons inhabited the rural tracts and gave no space either to scriptures or religious codes in their daily lives. More concerned with solving real life problems rather than enquiring into their causes the simple minded villagers turned to a variety of sacred resources, evil spirits and sorceresses to rescue them or grant their wishes.

It may be pointed out that Ruchi Ram Sahni's drive for popularisation of science in this region could not ignore the dominant presence of peasant culture even among the Western educated urban elite. A few empirical details about Punjab will clarify the point. Punjab was predominantly an agrarian society in the nineteenth century. In 1881, 87 per cent of its population lived in 34,000 villages and only 13 per cent in urban centres.[5] The rulers and the ruled (except a small number of mercantile families) were dependent on income from agricultural production. The colonial rule in Punjab did not dramatically alter the situation. Denzil Ibbetson, who had been associated with Punjab in various official roles, recorded that this region had neither vast towns and cities like Calcutta and Bombay nor great fatories nor varied mineral wealth.[6]

For much of the nineteenth century, the majority of the Punjabis continued to live in an 'enchanted universe' to use Max Weber's phrase.[7] Dotted with shrines of *pirs* or *saints, jatheras* or clan ancestors, temples of disease-goddesses and other local godlings,[8] the Punjabi countryside attracted devotees from towns and cities. Among their devotees were included a large number of Sikhs, Hindus and Muslims. The explanation of their fervent faith in the miraculous powers of *Sakhi Sarvar, Gugga Pir, Sitala Devi* or *Suraj Devta* may be found in the popular perception of natural calamities, illness, disease and healing. In the pre-industrial society of Punjab, the people tended to attribute floods, drought, fire, famines and illness to the anger of nature pantheon, malignant influence of a deity or to possession by an evil spirit or demon.

Let us take examples of physical afflictions. In a peasant society, crippling arthritis and chronic rheumatism of joints are highly prevalent. Working for long hours on agricultural chores and handling farming implements were major causes of physical deformities among the cultivators. The inventory of illnesses for which cures were sought included intestinal disorders, eye diseases particularly blindness, tetanus, leprosy, localised paralysis and psychosomatic disorders. As there was no well-developed public health system and medical science to treat diseases, psycho-social problems and to cure minor ailments, the unletteed peasants turned to supernatural forces, sorcerers, *ojhas, sianas* and astrologers.

Visits to the shrines of *pirs* (minor shrines) and *khankahs* (major shrines) formed part of standard curative practices. These shrines catered not only to the spritual needs of simple minded rural folks but also provided cures to invalids from different denominations whose afflictions had often unknown causes and an uncertain prognosis. In performing their roles as healers, the *mejaweri* (successors of pirs who managed the shrine) did not undertake to establish the *aetiology* of any disease but to administer cures. All diseases were not treated at the same shrine. There was a kind of specialisation among different pirs and their shrines. For example, the main *khankahs* (shrine) of Sakhi Sarovar at Dera Ghazi Khan had specialised in dealing with problems of spirit possession among women. The shrine of *Gugga Pir* at Bikaner, whose supernatural powers were invoked to grant wishes, heal the sick, protect cattle and bestow a son upon the devotee, specialised in curing his worshippers of snake and scorpion bites. Another example is of *Sitala Devi,* the goddess of pustular diseases who was worshipped all over Punjab by Hindus and Sikhs alike. Denzil lbbetson, the chief ethnographer of Punjab, has recorded the therapeutic rituals to appease the goddess in nineteenth century Punjab.

The observers of Punjabi society are struck by the absence of the confrontationist approach to nature among the rural (even urban) people in the nineteenth century.[9] One reason is the impact of cultural socialisation which inculcates a friendly and respectful attitude towards natural forces. The second reason is the availability of favourable ecological conditions on the whole as compared with the cold and harsh climates of European countries. Naturally, the Punjabi peasantry showed no inclination to control or dominate nature and their environment for individual and communal needs. That was why village gods were assigned important roles both in life cycle and agrarian cycle, particularly at the time of harvesting and sowing of crops. Apart from emotional bonds among their devotees, these godlings were instrumental in protecting them from diseases, threats from the outside world and evil spirits. For example, local godling Bhoomias, represented by a heap of stones and generally placed on the boundaries of a hamlet, was invoked to protect the land on which villages were settled.

Nature worship was also an important constituent of popular religion. In its pantheon was included Sun or the *Suraj Devta* as the major planet to be propitiated, the lesser ones being

Mercury and Mars. Earth was widely venerated as Mother, i.e. *Dharti Mata* because the rural folks were heavily dependent on fertile soil for abundant agricultural crops. Another god in this pantheon was Khwaja Khizr, the water god, who rules rivers and streams. His favours were invoked both for protection from floods and adequate water for irrigating fields. Evidently, the relationship between the local gods and peasantry, for whom the village and its immediate environment represented the entire cosmos, was crucial in his day-to-day experiences.

It may be conceded that the popular religion and priestly religion had worked out a comfortable relationship over the centuries, implicating a process of mutual give and take. With the growth of the middle classes under the colonial rule, the reciprocal influence of the cultures of the powerful and the subordinate acquired a new angle. The popular culture, especially the oral tradition of the numerically dominant peasant population, circulated freely in the small towns and the big cities through the English educated sons of the village literati who acted as a bridge between the priestly elite culture of the urban areas and the rural culture.

Interestingly, this generation of the new elite also represented the rationalist critique and offensive against the Brahminical domination and excesses, rigid social hierarchies based on caste as well as against superstitious faith in magic cures, saint cults and sacred sites associated with village religion. Influenced by the enlightenment ideology, they tended to regard science as the 'pioneer instrument' for all progress.[10] The socio-religious reformers of the period also shared faith in scientism and used it as a weapon to counter missionary attacks upon their religions—be it Hinduism, Islam or Sikhism. Without going into the details of the reform process, I wish to emphasise that rationalists like Ruchi Ram Sahni and Mahendra Lal Sircar, who were trained as scientists, tried to understand the nature of their societies wherein they had sought to popularise science.

Ruchi Ram Sahni, well-known commentator on Punjabi society, colonial culture and national policies, informs us that the religious boundaries were not rigidly drawn in nineteenth century Punjab. Even in the urban areas, most of the people did not see any clash between the tenets of Hinduism and Sikhism. Recalling his formative years, he observed, 'my religious beliefs were as fragile and indefinite as that of my father, but in my case at least there was a distinct leaning towards the tenets of Sikhism'.[11] He worshipped idols and recited *Rehras* and *Sukhmani* with equal fervour. Ruchi Ram Sahni attributed the prevailing ambivalence towards religion to liberal socialisation in the family rather than scientific or rational thinking. The accommodative spirit of the Punjabis owed in large measure to the absence of Brahminical dominance in a peasant society which valued the Jats for their utility in an agricultural economy, despite their low status in the religious hierarchy. It was reinforced by the egalitarian teachings of Sikhism and their large scale conversion to the new creed.

II

Gearing Towards Change: The New Social Forces

The foregoing description of mid-nineteenth century Punjab has underlined the prevalence of polytheism, superstitions supernaturalism, a diluted version of the caste system in the absence of socio-economic ascendancy of Brahmins and the other discriminatory social practices. This conservative social environment, which had slowed the pace of innovation in thought and practice including science and technology, was to experience tensions when exposed to European ideologies and institutions. Among the various catalytic agents, which affected the mindset and behaviour of the Punjabis, the major ones were the Western educational institutions, print culture and the Brahmo ideology.

The first major catalyst was the Western education system, introduced with a two-fold objective : utilitarian and ideological. Macaulay and many of his contemporaries believed that military conquest had only won them a precarious hegemony. The most enduring and the profitable conquest was over the mind. It acquired even more urgency in the case of Punjab which had to be controlled through conquest over the hearts and minds of its inhabitants especially the social and economic elites. The colonial mission was an instant success as the first generation of Indian intelligentsia in nineteenth century Bengal began to believe that it was only through the medium of English education that the reservoir of European scientific knowledge would be open to them. Raja Ram Mohan Roy and many of his contemporaries, regarded Britain as the chosen instrument for leading India to the path of political and economic modernisation.[12]

The British rulers were keen that this ideological perspective should be effectively publicised in the recently annexed Punjab which had to be converted into a secure but also profitable possession. Obviously, a serious missionary effort for the spread of Western education, including literary and scientific, was made in order to colonise the consciousness of Punjabis.[13]

Lahore was chosen as the centre for administrative and educational institutions. By early 1870, it had developed into a typical colonial metropolis and by the 1880s became the hub of the cultural life of the north.[14] Possessing abundant resources, imperial aura, educational facilities and employment opportunities, it attracted young Punjabis thirsting for new knowledge in arts and science, eager to experiment with new gifts of the raj and willing to embark upon new careers. Many among them like Ruchi Ram Sahni, Lala Lajpat Rai, Gurmukh Singh and Bhagat Lakshman Singh were destined to become prominent intellectuals while others earned educational degrees in the hope of prosperous futures but lived in anonymity.[15]

These new intellectual elites were the product of a network of Western educational institutions including anglo-vernacular schools of arts and science and engineering and medical colleges in Lahore, and other cities and towns of Punjab. The opening of the first Government school in 1851 at Amritsar was followed by a chain of such institutions at Rawalpindi, Gujrat, Shahpur, Multan, Jhelum and Jalandhar. By 1856, there were thirty-five such schools.[16]

The next major landmark in the development of Western education in Punjab was the opening of Government College in Lahore in 1864 which taught courses in Arithmetic, Algebra, Euclidean Trigonometry, Conic Sections, Logic, Economics,

English, Persian, History, Physics and Chemistry. Under the principalship of G.W. Leitner the college emerged as a major educational institution. It was here that Ruchi Ram Sahni, first as a student and later as a faculty member, was drawn to the Western scientific ideas. His concerns and sensibilities, particularly a real love and admiration for the English language as a noble vehicle of thought and feeling,[17] matured in the company of his fellow students. As a student he also demonstrated his passion for Western scientific knowledge, technologies and his ability to improvise cheap alternatives for experiments and lantern slide demonstrations for public lectures.

The second Western innovation was the printing technology which had facilitated the exchange and circulation of books like any other commodity. Described as *'print culture'* by McLuhan,[18] such a phenomenon transformed the Punjabi society which was based on oral and scribal knowledge, into a society where printing technology became crucial for the reproduction of ideas and knowledge. Thus, the printed word became not only a source of ideas and images but also a bridge between scholars, scientists, students, social reformers and rural gentry. Easy availability of books, tracts, journals and newspapers had excited the imagination of students who could go beyond the prescribed textbooks and familiarise themselves with European ideas on liberty, humanism and rationalism.

The eager students of Government College, Lahore, spent their leisure time in discussing, examining and scrutinising the implications of social theories and relevance of European ideas and scientific knowledge for shaping modern India. In his memoirs, Ruchi Ram Sahni recorded an illustration of one such stimulating reading session.[19]

> The remarkable books, as they appeared both to Guru Dutt and myself, we also read together in our spare hours in the college veranda, or rather the vestibule. These were Mill's 'Utilitarianism' and Bentham's 'Theory of Legislation'. They were, of course, not included in the college 'Course', but that was of little consideration for both of us. We read and re-read Mill's small book line by line, or paragraph by paragraph ...

> Now and again, we could not do more than a sentence or two in the course of an hour, for either we could not agree as to what the author's real meaning was, or for some reason, the whole time was taken up with discussion about all the implications of the passage or how far we could accept his lead. Now and again, we would deliberately take up our stand on opposite sides, so as to be able to thrash our point as well as we could. As on such occasions, we would, as a rule, undertake to support the experimental view-point while Guru Dutt would become the exponent of the *Transcendental* school...... sometimes 'these discussions were attended by elderly persons from the city interested in one or other of the contestants. Now and again, the debates became quite animated and heated, each party pleading for his own thesis'.

Obviously, these eager students, who matured under the influence of the enlightenment ideology during the 1880s and 1890s, had evinced a great admiration for Europe's achievement in literature, political theory and practice of democracy, positivism, scientific knowledge and technology. Their intellectual growth acquired more flesh when they came into contact with the English educated Bengalis in Lahore who had already internalised the discourse of scientific rationality of the raj. The earliest evidence of the application of modern scientific rationality to reform Indian society is found in Raja Ram Mohan Roy's *Tuhfat-ul-Mowahidin* (1803) wherein he has tried to define a rational theology.[20]

The third important catalyst of the socio-cultural milieu in Punjab was the Bengali Brahmo community which had provided a large number of clerks, teachers, pleaders and doctors as the human underpinning of the raj. Having crystallised as a social force, it played a crucial role not only in altering the traditional social and economic hierarchy but also in changing habits of the mind among the literate classes. During the 1880s, Brahmo Samaj and its creed was the major ideological influence on Punjabis, particularly Hindu consciousness. Ruchi Ram Sahni became a regular member of the Brahmo Samaj within a couple of years after his arrival at Lahore as a student in October, 1879. Among the other young men who turned to the Brahmo Samaj, included Devi Chand Gupta (better known as Shradha Prakash Deva), Bhai Sunder Singh, Bhai Harbhagwan, Bhai Chatter Singh, Pandit Girdhar Raj Biswasi and Chander Prakash Deva.

Ruchi Ram Sahni's decision to study science and assume the role of a cursader for scientific awareness was influnced to some extent by his close involvement in Brahmo Samaj activities in Lahore. To the Bengali Brahmo intelligentsia and their Punjabi brethren-in-faith like Ruchi Ram Sahni, science connoted certain values: unity over diversity, the compilation and successful application of useful knowledge about men, society and the universe, the search of natural laws, optimism about the vital role of science in progress.[21] Brahmos not only appropriated science and rationalism in a special way but also deified them. Brahmo scientists were the first modern scientists in contemporary India particularly in Bengal.

Most Indians, especially Punjabis, despite their resentment against the domination of the Bengali Brahmo elite in educational and administrative institutions of the raj and religious life for almost half a century, continued to regard Calcutta as an intellectual centre. For many of them including Ruchi Ram Sahni, residence in a big city like Calcutta was in itself a 'continuous source of education'.[22] It proved to be useful in two ways. Firstly, his interest in chemistry grew into a passion under the inspiring guidance of Professor Sir Alexander Pedler in the classroom and laboratory of the local Presidency College where he was a student. While assisting his teacher in his work as an analyst to the Calcutta Municipality, Ruchi Ram acquired training in testing wines and methodical preparation of reports in a short time. As a student, he had not only formed a lifelong association with his aforesaid intellectual mentor but also with his class fellow Ashutosh Mookerjee who rose to be the Vice-Chancellor, Calcutta University later on.[23] Upendra Kishore Roy Choudhary, his class fellow in the M.A., strengthened his Brahmo sympathies. Secondly, the idea of his future role as a crusader for scientific awareness crystallised while listening to the public lectures of Professor Jagadish Chandra Bose, P.C. Ray and Father E. Lafont in the Indian Association for the

Cultivation of Science, Calcutta.[24] This Institute's role inspired Ruchi Ram to set up the Punjab Science Institute in collaboration with Professor J.C. Oman, his colleague in Government College Lahore in the summer of 1885.

III

Ruchi Ram Sahni's Crusade for Scientific Awareness

Dissemination of scientific awareness in a colonial society implied theoretical understanding of the subject, ability for its practical application and demonstration and a talent for lucid transmission of factual knowledge to the people with an average intelligence in their own idiom. Even more serious was the lack of organisational/institutional structure to aid the popularisation of science among the people. Establishment of as many as 170 colleges including several medical and engineering colleges and technical education institutions (affilliated to the five universities—Calcutta, Madras, Bombay, Lahore and Delhi) and ten scientific services had only trained and employed Indians as clerks, second-rank technicians, and engineers to run railways, shipping or canal construction ventures or to gather information about botanical, zoological and mineral resources.[25] Transfer and relocation of Western scientific knowledge and technologies was only partly successful in terms of long-term benefits to the Indian people. It was so because these ventures were conceived of and remained as mere technological projects which did not target at diffusion of knowledge and skills. Indians were educated to a certain point and culture of technology was withheld from them.[26] As colonial subjects, non-Europeans including Indians were denied opportunities for enterprise, investment and experience. It is evident from Rai Bahadur Ganga Ram's bitter experience who was discouraged not only from making investment on lift-irrigation technology to harness water near Renala in Lower Bari Doab canal but also deprived of a contract to construct tube-wells on his plot in Upper-Chenab Colony.[27]

Painfully aware of the conflict between the colonial agenda of scientific development and needs as well as aspirations of the Indians, Ruchi Ram Sahni launched his mission for the transfer of scientific knowledge and grafting of technologies. It was difficult for any Indian to get state patronage or funding for projects concerned with dissemination of scientific awareness. Hence, paucity of financial resources made Ruchi Ram Sahni's task as a crusader for scientific awareness, indeed, daunting.

Despite all these handicaps, Ruchi Ram Sahni took the first step towards his goal by establishing the Punjab Science Institute in 1885.[28] The idea of this institute had originated with Professor J.C. Oman but it took a concrete shape after Sahni had seen the working of the IACS. Founded in mid-1885 with Professor Oman as Honorary Secretary and Sahni as Joint Secretary, the original aim and object of the Punjab Institute was the popularisation of all kinds of scientific knowledge throughout the province by means of lectures (in English and vernacular) illustrated with experiments and lantern slides, as well as the publication of tracts. These objects, according to Ruchi Ram Sahni, were expanded to include the encouragement of technical education, and, in particular of chemical industries.

In pursuance of the original object of science popularisation Ruchi Ram Sahni managed to involve several Professors from local colleges in the activities of the Institute especially in its lecture-programme. For example, Professor Oman delivered several lectures on various aspects of 'Electricity' and 'Magnetism'. Dr. C.C. Caleb, who was on the faculty of Medical College, Lahore, gave a series of lectures on human anatomy. Caleb's two lectures 'Man's Fear' and 'Smokes: Poisonous and Non-poisonous', became especially popular. Dr. Grant's lectures on 'Soap Bubbles', 'Chemical History of the Candle' and 'Spinning Tops' were particularly well-received. Sahni himself gave as many as five hundred popular lectures in various towns of Punjab and repeated these in private gatherings on personal invitation from local elites. His lectures on weather with special reference to India were based on sound and practical knowledge which he had acquired in the course of his job as the second Assistant Meterological Reporter to the Government of India.

Public lectures arranged by the Punjab Science Institute

aroused tremendous interest among the residents of Lahore, especially among students who had enlisted their parents as active supporters of the Institute. As a result, Sahni received invitations for lectures from the *rais* of Patiala, Kapurthala, Mandi and Bahawalpur. Besides, he used to give a regular annual course of twenty lectures on the basic facts and principles of Physics and Chemistry to the large audiences, consisting entirely of shopkeepers. Ten lectures were devoted to general topics such as 'How Does the Telegraph Wire Speak', 'The Common Flame', 'Electroplating', 'Electricity in the Service of Man' (a series of three or four lectures), 'Glass Making' and 'Punjab and its Rivers'. The last one was illustrated by a large relief map of India (Made in clay under Sahni's direction for an Educational Exhibition at Lahore). Several of these lectures, especially those giving advance information, were repeated in Lahore city itself and also in a few small towns. Ruchi Ram's tireless crusade for the popularisation of science created 'a real furore of enthusiasm in the province about scientific studies.'

Indeed, the personal commitment and concerted efforts of Ruchi Ram Sahni and his associates, particularly Professor Oman and Dr. Caleb, had succeeded in arousing interest in popular science among the people. The Punjab Science Institute, which was substituted by the newly established Society for the Promotion of Scientific Knowledge, founded by local Medical College students in 1905, had been able to raise a substantial amount of funds owing to the good quality of lectures, illustrated by practical demonstrations and lantern slides.[30] It may be mentioned that Sahni had reinforced his mission by the establishment of the Punjab Science Institute Workshop. However, there is no evidence to suggest that enthusiasm and interest in popular science, which Ruchi Ram Sahni had generated so assiduously, matured into a science movement in this region.

Another aspect of Ruchi Ram Sahni's contribution was to underline the positive role of regional languages in the dissemination of scientific knowledge among the masses. Despite the fact that perceptions of the educated elites in Punjab during the 1880s had been influenced by the Brahmo leaders of the Bengal renaissance, they had increasingly turned to indigenous sources for inspiration and strength as the century drew to its close.[31] Hence, Punjabi was assigned a valuable role for social and intellectual regeneration. Ruchi Ram Sahni also preferred the use of Punjabi as a vehicle for scientific knowledge in his popular lectures. Judging by the response of his audience including average men and elites, Sahni concluded that the mother tongue was the best medium to communicate knowledge of modern science. It would enable the people to adapt scientific knowledge and technologies to their environment and finally contribute to the development of alternate technologies. That the local languages were best suited to the fruitful dissemination of scientific knowledge among the masses was a deep-rooted conviction common among Indian intellectuals such as Raja Ram Mohan Roy, Master Ram Chandra and his contemporary Sir Syed Ahmed Khan. There was a definite political agenda underlying the translation of the best European writings into Indian languages. Sir Syed Ahmed Khan pleaded that:[32]

> Those bent on improving and bettering India must remember that the only way of compassing this is by having the whole of arts and sciences translated into their languages.

The strongest argument in favour of the translation project was that the constant use of English language by impressionable children would not only habituate them to express their thoughts in it but also 'denationalise' them. Both Master Ramchandra and Ruchi Ram Sahni had expressed their anxious concern for the alienation of the younger generation whose patriotic feelings ought to be nurtured. Both of them had actively contributed to the building of 'national character'.[33] While the former devoted his energy and talent to the translation of a number of European works on science in Urdu, the latter popularised information about the latest inventions and various branches of scientific knowledge through his lectures in Punjabi, the most widely spoken language in this region.

IV

Conclusion

A review of Ruchi Ram Sahni's contribution towards the spread of scientific awareness among the common people living in the urban areas (lecture-tours to villages being very few) draws our attention to three crucial issues (i) relationship between religion and science, (ii) tension between the practice of nationalism and cultivation of Western science and technology, and (iii) conflict between the agenda of colonial science and needs/aspirations of the subject people.

The first issue concerning the nature of relationship between science and religion, also addressed in Europe in the last decades of the eighteenth century and first half of the nineteenth century, does not necessarily imply conflict, but a half-way meeting of two human initiatives (seemingly opposed) to maximise social progress, welfare and happiness. Both the scientist and the social reformer in colonial India had sought to achieve this shared objective through the pursuit of knowledge and scientific rationality. While the scientists of Ruchi Ram Sahni's generation were engaged in acquiring 'superior' and modern scientific knowledge and technologies for nation building, the social reformers had chosen to mediate the recovery and return to Upanishadic or Vedic knowledge. In their critique of Indian cultural tradition, social institutions and practices, religious codes and knowledge-systems as well as in their formulation of models and strategies for recasting society, economy and polity, impact of the West, particularly Comte's positivism, bourgeois values and concept of democracy, liberty, progress and modernity was obvious. Very often their roles overlapped. Both of them had used rationalism as a major argument for denuding Hinduism of its excrescences : idol-worship, superstitions, blind faith in demons' spirits, caste distinctions and outdated religious rituals as well as for popularising Western scientific knowledge and technologies.

Ruchi Ram Sahni, whose thought process had largely been influenced by the Brahmo intellectuals particularly Jagadish Bose and Prafulla Chandra Ray, had sought to resolve the conflict between the Western scientific rationality and intuition-oriented Indian religions by turning to the Brahmo Samaj. Without rejecting the need and support of religion, he practised rational theology. After joining the Brahmo Samaj as a regular member, he had discarded the sacred thread—the cherished mark of a high caste orthodox Hindu. His commitment to rationalism was demonstrated when he had parted with his Brahmo mentor Shiv Narain Agnihotri because the latter indulged in self-glorification as a godman of sorts. Thus, scientific rationality had been used as a tool for bringing about socio-cultural change not only by Ruchi Ram Sahni but by the Brahmo ideologies generally.

The second issue concerning tension between the practice of nationalism and cultivation of Western scientific knowledge was viewed by the Brahmos from a different angle. For example, Jagadish Bose who believed in Brahmo-inspired universalism, argued that knowledge was not the monopoly of any race and thus '...science is neither of the East nor of West but international'. Most of the Indian scientists sincerely believed that universalism and unity of knowledge were crucial to the growth of civilisation and common heritage of mankind. However, their bitter experiences as colonial subjects obliged them to confront the cultural chauvinism of the British imperialists who claimed scientific genius and achievements as the prerogative of the Anglo-Saxon races and behaved arrogantly. For example, Ruchi Ram Sahni has recounted the blatant form of racial discrimination against Indians in daily life. His personal experience of supercession in the Educational Service in addition to the frequent humiliations as an individual not only angered him but also enabled him to evolve his own code of conduct to live with dignity.

Despite wilful denial of opportunities of training, professional growth and promotion by the colonial state, the national-minded scientists neither boycotted scientific institutions and services nor honorific titles. They channelised their frustration and anger into a more creative way like (i) creation of scientific awareness among adults and improving quality of science teaching in schools, (ii) opening of *swadeshi* chemical industries and scientific workshops and (iii) translation of Western scientific works into vernacular languages. These three forms highlight the common trend of thinking—harnessing training and Western scientific knowledge for nation-building indirectly. It was an acknowledgement of the scientific achievements of the European nations and the keen desire of their colonial subjects to emulate them without abandoning their civilisation.

The third issue concerns the conflict between the agenda of colonial science and needs/aspirations of the Indian people. The colonial rulers perceived three potential roles for science. Its first role was concerned with exploration and discovery, the second with solving environmental and disease problems and the third with providing ongoing advice and technical services. All these roles targeted at making the colonies reproductive and at exploiting their potential in terms of human and natural resources as a tribute exacted from the hapless colonial subjects. Neither the development of the intellectual potentialities of the subject people nor economic modernisation of their country were on the agenda of the British rulers who had increasingly harnessed science and technology to holster the empire and capitalism. It was not only scientific education which was underdeveloped but research as well. Factually speaking, training of Indians as qualified doctors, engineers and scientists was not a priority for the British rulers because these ranks were always available to metropolitan graduates in the biological and other sciences. Directed by the colonial-administrators-turned-ethnographers, the British officers in scientific institutions and services constantly used scientific means for social control with a view to perpetuating political hegemony. The statistical population surveys are a good example.

The foregoing discussion has shown that scientists like Ruchi Ram Sahni had been obliged to negotiate between the pulls and pressures of their intense desire to modernise their society through the instrumentality of Western scientific knowledge and the patriotic compulsion to flight for the defence of the Indian cultural tradition and for national freedom. Despite role-conflicts and limited resources and space as a colonial subject, Ruchi Ram Sahni had tried to lay the foundation of modern scientific tradition through his campaign for popularisation of science. However, his pioneering initiative failed to mature into a science movement. Firstly, Ruchi Ram Sahni failed to train a team of students to continue either his task of popularisation of science or of improving quality of science teaching in schools. Those who were trained as scientists in this region were not farsighted enough to think beyond individual achievement. Secondly, the absence of large-scale industries also did not favour the growth of a science movement. Thirdly, the colonial state was not interested in the development of science in this region. But on the whole the examples set by Ruchi Ram Sahni in Punjab were in line with the current of 'limited modernisation' then passing in the local metropolis like Calcutta. Nevertheless, his crusade for the popularisation of science in Punjab had stimulated a great deal of interest in the pursuit of western knowledge without devaluing Indian cultural heritage and struggle for freedom.

REFERENCES

1. For an interesting discussion of cultural fermentation in 19th century Punjab see Kenneth W. Jones, 'The Bengali Elite in Post-Annexation Punjab: An Example of Inter-regional Influence in 19th Century India', *The Indian Economic and Social History Review*, III (4), December 1966, pp. 377-95.
2. Kamlesh Mohan, 'Colonialism and Ethnic Identities: 19th to Early 20th Century', in A J Qaisar and S.P. Verma, eds., *Art and Culture: Endeavours in Intepretation*, Delhi: Abhinav Publications, 1996), pp. 171-8.
3. I have borrowed this insight from John Hedley Brooke, *Science and Religion: Some Historical Perspectives*, New York: Cambridge University Press, *1991, 1993*, pp. 82-117.
4. S.J. Tambiah, *Buddhism and the Spirit Cults in North-East Thailand*, Cambridge: Cambridge University Press, 1970, pp. 371-7. On the basis of his study of three villages in Thailand, Tambiah has argued that 'the idea of two levels (of religion) is an invention of the anthropologist'. His suggestion of looking at a 'total field of religion' gives a more integrated view of society.
5. Denzil Ibbetson, *Census of Punjab, Report 1881*, Lahore;

Government Printing Press, 1883, p. 17.

6. D. Ibbetson, E.D. Maclagan, and H.A. Rose, *A Glossary of the Tribes and Castes of the Punjab*, Vol. I, Lahore; Govt. Printing Press, 1919, p. 3.
7. Max Weber, *The Religion of China: Confucianism, Lanism and Taoism*, New York: The Free Press of Glenoe, 1962, p. 226.
8. Description of saints, pirs, disease-goddesses, nature pantheon is based on various *Census Reports of Punjab* from 1881 to 1931; R.C. Temple, *Legends of Punjab*, 3 vols., Patiala, Language Department of Punjab 1962-63; first published 1884-86; David Kinsley, *Hindu Goddesses: Visions of the Divine Feminine in Hindu Religious Tradition*, (Berkeley: University of California Press, 1986 and David Gilmartin, 'Shrines, Succession and Sources of Moral Authority', in B.D. Metcalf, ed., *Moral Conduct and Authority*, Berkeley: California University Press, 1984, pp. 221-40.
9. Harjot Oberoi, *The Construction of Religious Boundaries: Culture, Identity and Diversity in the Sikh Tradition*, Delhi: Oxford University Press, 1994, p. 202.
10. Michael Worboys, 'Science and the Colonial Empire 1849-1940, in Deepak Kumar, ed., *Science and Empire*, Delhi: Anamika Prakashan, 1991.
11. Narender K. Sehgal and Subodh Mahanti, eds. *Memoirs of Ruchi Ram Sahni: Pioneer of Science Popularisation in Punjab*, New Delhi: Vigyan Prasar, 1994, p. 133.
12. K.N. Panikar, 'The Intellectual History of Colonial India : Some Historiographical and Conceptual Questions', in S. Bhattacharya and Romila Thapar, eds., *Situating Indian History*, Delhi: Oxford University Press, 1986, p. 421.
13. Charles Gough and Arthur D. Inner, *The Sikhs and the Sikh Wars*, First published 1897; Reprinted, Delhi : National Book Shop, 1984, p. 222.
14. For contemporary impressions about socio-cultural configuration of Lahore see Ved Mehta, *Daddyji*, Delhi: Oxford University Press, 1972, pp. 35-6; Ruchi Ram Sahni, 'Self-revealations of an Octogenarian' (Manuscript is lying with his grandson Professor Ashok Sahni, Panjab University, Chandigarh).
15. Bhagat Lakshman Singh, *Autobiography*, ed. Ganda Singh, Calcutta: The Sikh Cultural Centre, 1865, p. 133.
16. *Education Commission Report*, Calcutta: Government Printing Press, 1884, p. 8. Appendix contains the Report by the Punjab

Provincial Committee with Evidence Taken Before the Committee and Memorials addressed to the Commission.

17. Ruchi Ram Sahni, 'Self-Revelations of an Octogenarian', *op. cit.*, note 14, p. 128.
18. M. McLuhan, *The Gutenbery Galaxy*, London: Routledge and Kegan Paul, 1962.
19. Ruchi Ram Sahni, 'Self-Revelations of an Octogenarian', op. cit., note 14, p. 139.
20. Cited in K.N. Panikkar, 'Presidential Address' to the 36th Session of the Indian History Congress, 1975, Section III,
21. David Kopf, *The Brahmo Samaj and the Shaping of the Modern Indian Mind*, Delhi: Archives Publishers Pvt. Ltd. in arrangement with Princeton University Press, U.S.A. 1988, p. 48
22. Ruchi Ram Sahni, *Memoirs*, op. cit., note 11, p. 11.
23. Details about Sahni's associates in Calcutta are contained in his *Memoirs*, op. cit., note. 11, pp. 5-12.
24. Mahendralal Sircar qualified in Medicine in 1860 from the Medical College Caluctta and received the M.D. degree in 1863. In 1876, he founded the Indian Association for the Cultivation of Science, the first institute for scientific research in India. He was a member of the Bengal Legislative Council from 1887 to 1893.
25. R.M. McLeod, 'Scientific Advice for British India: Imperial Perception and Administrative Goals 1898-1923', *Modern Asian Studies*, 9(3), 1975, pp. 343-84. Ten scientific services included the Meteorological Reporter, The Inspector General of the Civil Veterinary Department, the Director of-the Botanical Survey of India, The Reporter on Economic Products, The Inspector General of Agriculture, The Director General of Archaeology, The Chief Inspector of Mines, The Surveyor General, The Inspector General of Forests and The Director of Geological Survey.
26. Ian Inkster, 'Prometheus Bound: Technology and Industrialisation in Japan, China and India Prior to 1914: A Political Economy Approach', *Annals of Science*, 45, 1988, pp. 422-3.
27. Imran Ali, *The Punjab Under Imperialism 1885-1947*, Delhi: Oxford University Press, 1989, pp. 218-22.
28. My information regarding the establishment of the Punjab Science Institute, its objects and activities for the popularisation of science is based on Ruchi Ram Sahni, *'Self-Revelations'*, op. cit., note 14, pp. 256-67.
29. Ibid., p. 264.

30. For details of Ruchi Ram Sahni's improvisations for making photographic lantern slides, see his '*Self-Revelations*', pp. 259-61.
31. The renaissance in Punjab shares this feature with the Delhi Renaissance. For a detailed discussion of the role of vernacular in the Delhi Renaissance see Gail Minault, 'Sayyid Ahmed Dehalvi and the Delhi Renaissance', in R.E. Frykenberg ed., *Delhi Through the Ages*, Delhi: Oxford University Press, 1987, pp. 289-90.
32. Shan Mohammad, ed., *Writings and Speeches of Sir Syed Ahmed Khan*, Bombay: Asia Publishing House, 1972, pp. 231-2.
33. Both Munshi Zakaullah, a student of Master Ramchandra in Delhi, and Akshay Kumar Dutt had shown acute awareness of and concern for the consequences of the English education, especially its role in alienating young students from their own national culture.

Index

1857 revolt 32

academic discourse 2
adaptation and revitalisation 16
Africa 29, 31, 39, 41, 61
Agassiz, Louis 42
Aggarwals 55, 60
Agnihotri, Shiv Narain 149
Ali, Imdad 16, 18
Ali, Mumtaz 16
Ali, Aaulana Safdar 115
Aligarh Scientific Society 18
Aligarh University 96
Allahabad 13
Allahabad University 94
Ambedkar, B.R. 61
American University 81
American Bible and Tract Society 114
American scholars 61, 93
Anand, Chetan 73-4
Anderson, B. 29
Anglicist-Orientalist controversy 69
Anglo-Saxon races 31, 39, 98
Ankeny-Artin-Chowla theorem 93
Arya leadership 125
Arya reformers 123
Arya Sabha 118
Arya Samaj 121
  experiment 114
  movement 116, 119, 125
Aryans 48-9, 57
Asia 29, 39, 41, 61
Asian social systems 61
Asiatic Society of Bengal 9-10, 86, 95
Auluck, F.C. 93
Ayurvedic system of medicine 87

Baber, Zaheer 6
Bambah, R.P. 92-3
Banaras Hindu University 73, 87, 89, 91-2
Barbados 40
Barry, Lala Rattan Chand 121
Bashir Ahmad 91
Battle of Plassey 32
Behl, Karm Narayan 95
Bengal 8, 107
Bengali Brahmo community 142
Bengali Brahmo elite 143
Bengalis 113
  in Lahore 142
Bentinck, William 12
Bhabha, H.J. 96
Bhakti movement 110

Bhalla, Narinder Singh 94
Bhatia, Behari Lal 75
Bhatnagar, Shanti Swarup 77, 88, 90
Bihar 107
Bihar Scientific Society 18
Bingley, Captain A.H. 55
biodiversity 9
biological determinism 36, 41
Blanford, Sir H.F. 82
Bombay 14, 69, 70, 81, 144
Bombay Presidency 12, 75
Bose, Jagadish Chandra 82, 98, 143
Bose, R.C. 93
botanical gardens 9
botanical plants 4
Boulenger, C.L. 77
Brahmin-centred classification 56
Brahminical dominance 139
Brahminical domination and excesses 138
Brahmins 54-5
Brahmo ideology 139
Brahmo intellectuals 148
Brahmo leaders 146
  of the Bengal 83
Brahmo Samaj 105, 143, 149
Brahmo-inspired universalism 98
Britain 1-2
British census 7
British control 5
British Crown 34
British domestic politics 34
British East India Company regime 36
British educational policy 12, 80
British empire 32
British ethnographers-cum-administrators 55
British ethnological writings 49
British Government 14
British imperialism 56
British imperialist rulers 80
British imperialists 6
British India 6, 8, 17, 53
British policy 10
British political authority 36
British political discourse 34
British Punjab 8
British rule 6, 12, 45
British rulers 38, 51, 140, 150
British University 81
British society 33, 37
Bruck-Chowla-Ryser Theorem 93
Buddha's image 107
Buddhism 3

Calcutta 13-4, 37, 69-70, 81-2, 143-4
  renaissance 17
Calcutta University 143
Caldwell 49
Caleb, C.C. 83, 145-6
Cambridge University 85
capitalist colonial state 13
Carey, William 115
caste 8
  and race 57
  identities in colonial ethnography 50
  system 58
castes and tribes 7
Caxton, William 110
Central Tibet 86
Chand, Lala Amir 125
Chatterji, Golak Nath 72
Chawla, Gopal Singh 72, 76
Chawla, Sarvadaman 72-3, 76, 92-3
Chhibber, H.M. 74-5
China 3, 108
Chinese books 107
Chinese emperors 108
Chowla-Mordell theorem 93

Chowla-Selberg formula 93
Christian 123
missionaries 19, 41, 112-3, 117
orphanages 114
Christianity 11
civilisational discourses 31-2
Clark, Robert 116
class-hierarchies in Britain 4
classical languages 13
Clive 35
Cohn, Bernard S. 11, 56
College for Oriental Studies 71
colonial administrative 6
colonial administrators 30, 44, 74
and policy-makers 7, 29
colonial discourse 31
colonial elite 35
colonial ethnographic practice 7
colonial ethnography 49, 60
in British India 30
colonial exploitation and polarisation 33
colonial India 4, 69
colonial institutions 121
colonial knowledge 6
colonial modernity 16
colonial people 39
colonial power 37
colonial scientific societies 9
colonial set-up in India 81
colonial society 19
colonial subject 11
colonialism 39, 41, 113, 134
Combe, George 42
commercial 'races' 60
communitarian consciousness 61
Compton, Arthur Holy 96
Cornwallis 32
Counters, G.M. 96
Crank, W.H. 72
criminal tribes 55, 60
criminal tribes of South India 50
Crooke, W. 44, 48
Crown from the mid-nineteenth century 31
Crown rule 2
cultural and intellectual engineering 15, 134
cultural and symbolic order 35
cultural boundaries 8
cultural chauvinism of the British people 38
cultural discourse 35
cultural distinctiveness 19
cultural encounter 2
cultural hegemonisation 18
cultural hegemony 15
cultural roots 8
cultural socialisation 137
Curier, George 42

D.A.V. College 76
Dalal, Sir Ardeshir 91
Darwin, Charles 43
Delhi 76, 107, 123, 144
Delhi renaissance 17
Delhi University 94-5
democracy 142
development and modernisation 134
Devnagari script 116
dialogic potentialities 18
Dionne, Russel 4
Donovan, F.G. 89-90
Dravidians 49
Duncliff, H.B. 77

East India Company 2, 5, 11, 44, 112
in Calcutta 4
East Pakistan 57
East Panjab University 80
economic exploitation 35

economic forces 32
Edney, Mathew H. 5
educational movement 20
egalitarianism 37
Elphinstone, Mountstuart 36
Embree, Ainslie 5
English and Western sciences 13
English education in India 36
English language 71
English-knowing Indians 36
enlightenment ideology 142
enlightenment philosophy 15
Enthoven, R.E. 48
ethical superiority 31
ethnographic surveys 29
Europe 8
European anthropology 44
European colonial expansion 41
European history 37
European intellectual paradigm 40
European intellectual tradition 45
European knowledge 11-3
European racism 41
European rationalism 31, 33
European rationalist 38
    discourse 29
    theory 34
European scientific knowledge 37, 140
European scientific rationality 18
European scientists 16
European thinkers 15
European works 18
European writings into Indian languages 84

Falcon, Captain R.W. 55
financial investment 4
Flower, W.H. 47
Focault 51
foreign domination 15
Forman Christian College, Lahore 76, 79, 87, 96

G.S. Ghurye 57
Gait, E.A. 48
Gall, Franz Joseph 42
Galton, Francis 47
Gandhi, M.K. 61
Garrett, H.L.O. 74
Georgian Enclosure 43
Ghalib, Mirza 16
Ghosh, Rabindra Narayan 19
Giddon, George 42
Gill, Piara Singh 95-6
Godbole, N.N. 88
Goebel 85
Goodfellow, S. 12
governance 2
Government College, Lahore 70, 72, 74, 76-8, 81-2, 84, 87, 92, 98, 141, 144
Grant, Charles 11, 13, 83
Gujarat 57, 107, 110, 118
Gupta, H. 93
Gurmukhi script 115

Habib, Irfan 108
Hali, Altaf Hussain 16
Haque, Sir Azizul 91
Haryana 121
Hastings 35
hegemonic discourse 34, 36, 45
hegemonic strategies of the colonial state 14
hegemony 29
    strategies for 34
Hemmy, A.S. 73-4
Hindus 7, 19, 48, 55-6, 111, 118, 120-01, 123, 136
    and Muslims 49
    and Sikhs 8
    cultural backwardness of 116

consciousness 114, 123
of religion 106
Muslim culture 19, 49
religion 53
society 124
tradition 122
Hinduism 14, 18, 119, 138-9, 148
Hindustanis 113
Hobsbawm, E.J. 7
Hora, Sunder Singh 95
human resources 9
humanism and rationalism 141
humiliation 15
Hussain, Mian Afzal 78
Hussain, Mohammed Sarfaraz 18
Hutton, J.H. 30, 48

Ibbetson, Denzil 30, 56
ideological rationalisation 34
imperial 'hegemony' 7
imperialism and colonialism 1
imperialism and expansionism 39
imperialist expansion 32
imperialist rule in India 2
imperialist rulers 11
imperialist strategy for hegemony 1
India 1-2, 5-6, 31, 33, 93
cultural and intellectual heritage of 68
Indian Botanical Society 86
Indian classical languages 6
Indian Education Service in 1920 85
Indian history and civilisation 37
Indian identity 61
Indian intellectuals 15
Indian intelligentsia 14-5, 37
Indian literature, ancient 109
Indian mathematicians 93
Indian politics 34
and society 35
Indian religions 14, 45, 149
Indian social structure 46
Indian society 9, 29, 32, 50-51, 53-4, 58-9, 60, 69, 111, 113
Indian technology 33
Indian tradition of learning 16
Indianisation of Christianity 115
indigenous cultural and scientific traditions 16
indigenous knowledge 4, 13
indigenous structures 33
industrial capitalism 39
industrial revolution 43
industrialisation 37
intellectual campaign 5
intellectual realisation 17
Iqbal, Muhammad 78
Islam 18, 138
Islamia College 76

Jain, B.D. 91
Jesuit Missions 107
Jones, B. Mouat 73, 89, 98
Jones, Sir William 9-10, 114
Joseph Warren of Allahabad Mission 116
Joshi, Amar Chand 86-7
Joshi, S.S. 91

Kanes, Lord 41
Kapur, Inder Sen 94
Karve, Iravati 57
Kashmir 107
Kashyap, Shiv Ram 75-8, 84, 86-7
Khalsa College, Amritsar 86
Khan, Sir Syed Ahmed 16-8, 84, 118, 147
Khatri, Munshi Kanshi Ram 115
Kitchlew, Pratap Krishan 93, 95
knowledge systems in India 16
Krishna, Lord 110

Kshatriyas 54, 56

labourers in plantations 4
Ladakh 86
Lafont, Father E. 82, 143
Lahore 68, 71, 76, 78, 85, 107, 144, 146
Lahore Arya Samaj 121, 127
Lake Mansarovar 86
Lal, Manohar 78
Lal, Munshi Pyare 88
land tenure systems 45
language and history 45
Law School 70-71
Leitner, G.W. 70, 141
Lewis, T.C. 72
liberalism 33
liberty 141
lifestyle 17
Lindsay, T.W. 72
literacy skills 121
Littlewood, J.E. 72
London University 89-90
lower and middling classes 43
Lubbock, Sir John 47
Ludhiana Mission 114
Lyall, Alfred 47-9

Macaulary, Lord T.B. 12, 38, 112, 139
MacLeod, Roy 4
Madras 14, 69-70, 81, 144
Mahalanbois, P.C. 57
Maharashtra 57, 118
Maine, Sir Henry 45, 47
majorities and minorities 8
Majumdar, D.N. 57
Malayalis 113
Malthus, Thomas 43
Maratha Peshwa 36
Marathas 113
marriage customs 49
Marwaris 55, 60
Master Ram Chandra 16-7, 84, 147
Mata Prasad 91
Mathai, G. 77
Mathur, K.N. 91
Maynard, Sir John 76
McLeod, Sir Donald 69
McLuhan, Marshall 105, 141
Mehra, Pran Nath 86-7
Metcalf, Charles 36
Mian, A.M. 93
middle classes 59, 133
    of Calcutta 36
Middle East 41
Middleton, L. 58
Mill, James 13, 141
minorities 55
Mookerjee, Ashutosh 82, 143
Mountain Kailas 86
Mudaliar, Sir A. Ramaswamy 91
Mueller, Max 47, 120
Mughal 123
    administration 35
    rulers 107-8
Mukerji, Rai Bahadur S.B. 72
multi-ethnic society 51
multi-religious society 16
Munro, Thomas 36
Muslim scholars 109
Muslims 7, 19, 50, 55, 107-09, 111, 114, 120, 123, 136
Myles, W.H. 77
Mysore 107

naked brutal force 29
nationalist forces 48
nationalist struggles 2
Nawab of Oudh 36
Nazir, A.R. 93
Nehru, Jawaharlal 61, 91, 96
Nesfield 56

New University of Panjab 86
Newton, John 114
North-Western Provinces (NWP) 7, 53-4
Nott, Joshia 39, 42
Nur Jahan 108

O'Donnel 49
O'Dwyer, Sir Michael 76
old ruling classes 32
O'Malley, L.S.S. 30, 49
Oman, J.C. 73, 81, 82, 144-5
Oriental College 70
Oriental languages 78
Oriental studies 71
Orientalism 30
Oudh 107

Pakistan 93
Panjab University, Lahore 69, 71-3, 77-80, 84-7, 90-5, 99
Panjab University College 70-1
Pant, Rashmi 7
Patna University 94
peasant society 136
Pedler, Alexander 82
physical attributes 8
Pillai, S.S. 93
political representation 8
politico-economics and cultural hegemonisation 15
positivism 142
post-colonial scholarship 2
Presbyterian missionaries 116
Prinsep, H.T. 12
Punjab 19, 80, 107, 110, 114, 118, 121, 123
Punjab Bible 114
Punjab Customary Law 52
Punjab Science Institute 144-5
Punjab, Socio-cultural Milieu of 135
Punjabis 18, 80, 84, 113, 121-2, 133, 136, 139, 142-3, 147
  Hindu 117
  scholars 115
  society 52
  socio-cultural environ-ment 19
  young men 81
Puri, Mohinder Prakash 94
Puri, Ved Prakash 94
purity-impurity criteria 49

Quit India Movement 80
Quran 109

race 8
racial typologising 40
Radhakrishnan, S. 92
radical difference 14
Raj, Lala Hans 119, 122
Rai, Lala Lajpat 119, 140
Rai, Pandit Harsukh 16
Rajagopalachari, C. 91
Rajputs 50, 55
Ram, Lala Khushi 73
Ram, Lala Salig 122
Ram, Rai Bahadur Ganga 97, 144
Rao, C.R. 57, 93
Rao, C.S. 92
Rao, C.V.H. 77
Rao, K. Ananda 93
rationalisation 43
rationalism 14, 33, 37, 148
rationalist connection 29
rationality 15
Ray, P.C. 82, 143
religion 19, 112
religion and caste 9
'religion' and 'caste' 7
religion in the colonial imagination 8

religious and cultural traditions 134
Religious Books Society 114
religious communities 7
religious hierarchy 139
religious sensibilities 18
Rennell, James 6
Retzius, Anders 42
revenue and tenurial system 32
Ripon, Lord 34
Risley, Herbert 8, 30, 42, 44, 46-8, 51-2, 56-7
Robinson, Francis 108
Roy Choudhary, Upendra Kishore 143
Roy, Raja Ram Mohan 17, 37, 61, 84, 140, 147
Roy, Upendra Kishore 82
Royal Botanical Gardens 9

Saha, Meghnad 94
Sahai, Parmeshari 88
Sahai, Raghu Nath 88
Sahni, Birbal 77, 82
Sahni, Ruchi Ram 17-8, 73-4, 76, 81, 83-4, 89, 98, 129, 133, 135, 138, 140, 142-6, 148, 151
Sakhi Sarovar 137
Salam, Abdus 92
Sapru, Tej Bahadur 90
Sastry, S. 93
Schein, Marcel 96
science and politics 2
science and technology 2-3, 9, 11, 16, 19
    in ancient India 10
sciences and arts 112
scientific and technological ascendancy 33
scientific hierarchies 11
scientific knowledge 14, 17-8, 68
    and technologies 3, 142
    in a colonial regime 81
    in Europe 6
    in India 80
    technology 1
scientific racism 41
scientific rationality 17
scientific teaching and research 14
scientific tools and methods 31
Sergeant, Sir John 80
Seth, T.N. 91
Shudras 54
Sikh intellectuals 117
Sikh rule 123
Sikhism 18, 138-9
Sikhs 7, 55, 111, 114, 120, 123, 136
Sime, J. 72
Singh, Gurmukh 140
Singh, B.K. 89
Singh, Balwant 91
Singh, Bawa Kartar 77
Singh, Bhagat Lakshman 140
Singh, D. 93
Singh, Hira 10
Singh, Kishen 10
Sircar, Mahendra Lal 18, 138
skilled workers 19
slave plantocracy 40
Smith, R. Saumerz 8, 53
social and cultural traditions 49
social and economic hierarchy 142
social control 8
social customs 7, 45, 51
social Darwinism 43
social Darwinist 41
social identity 7
social morphology 62
social reform leaders 114
social-cum-racial hierarchies 11
social-hierarchies 60
socio-cultural angle 32

socio-cultural institutions 15
socio-cultural milieu 15
socio-cultural universe 135
socio-religious reformers 116
sounds racist and unconvincing 3
South Indian Brahmin-non-Brahmin divide 49
south Indians 113
Spencer, Herbert 43
Spurzheim, Johan Gaspar 42
Srivastava, D.L. 91
Steiner, George 105
Stephenson, Captain J. 75
Stephenson, Colonel J. 77
Sultan, Tipu 36
Sultan Zain-ul-Abedin 107
Sultanate period 107
superstitions 17
Swami Dayanand 16, 106, 116-9, 123
Swarup, Lakshman 77
Sykes, William Henry 44

Tamils 113
Tata Institute of Fundamental Research 96
taxonomic systems 29, 38
technological artifacts and methods 2
technological innovations 15
technological projects 2
technology and religion 19
tensions and contradictions 15
Thurston, E. 30, 49
Tilak, Lokmanya 61
Topinard, Paul 47
traditional Indian system 109
traditional Punjabi society 121
Trevelyan, Charles E. 38
Tupper, C.L. 52

uniform postal system 2
United Provinces 113
United States (USA) 39, 42, 96
upper castes 57
Urdu 18, 147
Uttar Pradesh 57

Vaishyas 54, 56
varna 49
    principle 56
Vedic literature 110
Vidyarthi, Pandit Guru Dutt 119-20, 122, 124
Vijayaraghvan, T. 93

Wallace, Alfred R. 43
Weber, Max 136
West Bengal 57
Western civilisation and nations 38
Western culture 112
Western education 31, 34-8, 114
    in order 31
    system 139
Western Europe 32
Western Himalayas 86
Western historiography 61
Western sciences 4, 12, 15
    and technology 69
Western scientific knowledge 2, 15, 17, 150
    and technologies 16, 97
Western scientific rationality 149
Western systems of education 70
White, Charles 41
Williams, Monier 120
Wilson, H.H. 12
Wise, James 30
Wood, Charles 13
World War II 79, 90

Young Bengal group 37

Zakaullah, Munshi 16